THE WOODSTOCK SERIES
Popular Music of Today
Volume One
ISSN 0891-9585

THE BEACH BOYS
Southern California Pastoral

REVISED EDITION

by
Bruce Golden
California State University, San Bernardino

Updated by Paul David Seldis

BORGO PRESS / WILDSIDE PRESS

www.wildsidepress.com

To the Memory of
Dennis Wilson

Copyright © 1976, 1991 by Bruce Golden & Paul Seldis.

All rights reserved.

Library of Congress Cataloging-in-Publication Data

Golden, Bruce, 1933-
  The Beach Boys : Southern California pastoral / by Bruce Golden. — 2nd ed., rev. and expanded / updated by Paul David Seldis.
      p. cm. — (The Woodstock series, popular music of today, ISSN 0891-9585 ; no. 1)
  Discography: p.
  Bibliography: p.
  Includes index.
  ISBN 0-89370-359-1 : $22.95. — ISBN 0-89370-459-8 (pbk.) : $12.95
  1. Beach Boys. 2. Rock musicians—United States—Biography. I. Seldis, Paul David, 1958- . II. Title. III. Series.
ML421.B38G6 1991   90-2538
782.42166'092'2—dc20   CIP
[B]   MN

SECOND EDITION

CONTENTS

A Beach Boys Chronology	5
Foreword to the Second Edition	9
Introduction to the First Edition	12
1. "Surfin'" to *All Summer Long* (1962-1964)	17
2. *Beach Boys Today* to *Beach Boys Party* (1965)	27
3. *Pet Sounds* to *Holland* (1966-1973)	31
4. *Still Cruisin'* (1974-1990)	43
Afterword, by Dr. Bruce Golden	49
An Overview of Beach Boys Releases	51
Discography	55
Bibliography	80
Notes	84
Index to Song and Album Titles	87
Index to Individuals, Groups, and Subjects	94
About the Authors	104

A BEACH BOYS CHRONOLOGY

1941   Mike Edward Love born (March 15th); his parents are cousins to Murray and Audree Wilson.

1942   Brian Douglas Wilson is born to amateur songwriter Murray and Audree Wilson (June 20th). Al Charles Jardine born (September 3rd).

1944   Dennis Carl Wilson born to Murray and Audree Wilson (December 4th).

1946   Carl Dean Wilson born to Murray and Audree Wilson (Dec-ember 21st).

1961   Brothers Brian, Carl and Dennis Wilson, cousin Mike Love and Al Jardine form The Beach Boys in Hawthorne, California (Fall). "Surfin'"/"Luau" single released on Candix and X Records (December 8th). "Surfin'" debuts on KFWB Radio at number 33 (December 29th). First paid live performance by The Beach Boys, at a Richie Valens Memorial Dance; fee: $300 (December 31st).

1962   As part of a KMEN-Radio-sponsored "Deb-Teens" fashion show, The Beach Boys perform live at Harris' Department Store in San Bernardino, California (Spring). The Beach Boys, with David Marks replacing Al Jardine, sign recording contract with Capitol Records (Summer). "Surfin' Safari" hits number 14 on national record charts (October).

1963   *Surfin' U.S.A.* climbs to number 2 on national album charts (July). *Little Deuce Coupe* stays on the charts for 46 weeks, climbing as high as *Billboard's* number 4 (Fall). Brian Wilson quits touring; Al Jardine rejoins group; David Marks leaves (also Fall).

1964 The Beach Boys go on first international tour, a week-long trip to Australia (January). "I Get Around" hits number 1 on national charts; first Beach Boys number one single (July 4th). The Beach Boys go on first European tour (October). *The Beach Boys* climbs to number 1, becoming first Beach Boys number one album (December).

1965 A then-unknown recording artist named Glen Campbell briefly tours with the band (February). "Help Me, Rhonda" becomes band's second number 1 hit (April). Bruce Johnston joins the group (April 9th).

1966 "Good Vibrations" hits number one in England one week after its release (Fall). The Beach Boys go on a world-wide tour (also Fall). "Good Vibrations" hits number 1 in the U.S. (December 10th)

1967 Van Dyke Parks joins the group (Winter). Long-awaited, self-proclaimed "masterpiece" *Smile* officially aborted (May 2nd). *Smiley Smile* becomes first official release of Brother Records, a Beach Boys-formed subsidiary of Capitol Records (September 18th).

1968 While on a tour of the Southeast, a concert date in Memphis, Tennessee is cancelled because of feared racial violence following the assassination of Martin Luther King, Jr. (April). After a year of transcendental meditation with Maharishi Mahesh Yogi, The Beach Boys embark on a 17-day tour featuring the Maharishi. Billed the "Event of the Decade," the tour draws more security people than paying fans (May).

Following the Soviet invasion of Czechoslovakia, the band plays at a music festival in Prague (Fall). Originally written by cult leader and convicted murderer Charles Manson, "Never Learn Not to Love" is released as a "B" single with "Bluebirds Over the Mountain" (December 8th).

1969   The Beach Boys sue Capitol Records, who delete the group from their catalog, making it virtually impossible to purchase the band's older records (April 12th). Murray Wilson sells the Sea of Tunes catalogue containing all of Brian Wilson's compositions to Irving Almo Music, the publishing arm of A&M Records (November).

1970   The band signs with Warner Brothers Records (January).

1971   The group appears on stage with The Grateful Dead at the Fillmore Theater in New York City. Two months later they perform at the closing of the Fillmore (April 27th). The band plays at the May Day Antiwar Demonstration in Washington, D.C. (May 1st).
   ABC-TV broadcasts their concert live from New York City's Central Park (August 19th). The band performs at Carnegie Hall (September 24th).

1973   The Joffrey Ballet Company presents "Deuce Coupe," a Twyla Tharp ballet incorporating fourteen Beach Boys songs (Spring). Murray Wilson, father of three of the Beach Boys, dies of a heart attack (June 3rd).

1974   Boosted by heavy touring and a strong promotional campaign, *Endless Summer*, a Capitol re-release of the group's most popular songs, eventually goes number 1 and platinum (June 24th).

1975   *Rolling Stone* Magazine names The Beach Boys "Band of the Year." The group embarks on a twelve-city tour with Chicago, playing in front of more than 700,000 fans and grossing $7.5 million (May-June).

1976   The Joffrey Ballet Company presents "Deuce Coupe II" (Spring). Brian Wilson appears on stage in Oakland, California for the first time in seven years (July 2nd). The "Brian is back!" campaign garners cover stories in *Crawdaddy, New Times, People, Rolling Stone,* and the *Village Voice*, as well as features in *Newsweek, New West* and *TV Guide*.

NBC-TV broadcasts *The Beach Boys: It's O.K.* (August). Fifteenth anniversary concert at the Los Angeles Forum (December 31st). The First Edition of *The Beach Boys: Southern California Pastoral*, by Bruce Golden, is published by The Borgo Press.

1977 The Beach Boys leave Warner Brothers for CBS Records, receiving a $2 million advance bonus (March 1st).

1983 Following Interior Secretary Watt's labeling of them as the "wrong element," The Beach Boys appear at the White House, posing for photographs with President and Mrs. Reagan (July 17th). An intoxicated Dennis Wilson drowns while swimming in Marina Del Rey (December 28th).

1987 *The Beach Boys...25 Years Together* is broadcast on national television.

1988 The Beach Boys are inducted into the Rock 'n Roll Hall of Fame in Cleveland, Ohio. "Kokomo" is released with the film *Cocktail* and becomes the group's first number one hit in twenty-two years.

FOREWORD
To the Second Edition

When *The Beach Boys: Southern California Pastoral* was first published in 1976, author Bruce Golden felt that the band was riding a wave of nostalgia, the crest of which would soon break. And in many ways it has, with the group's members having experienced a variety of changes indigenous to any fourteen-year period of human existence. However, in tune with the indomitable surfer spirit of which the band has always sung, The Beach Boys have discovered other waves to ride, and they are as popular today as they have ever been, with sales bolstered by the release on compact disc of many of their earlier albums, with concerts selling out nationwide, and with their induction in 1988 into the Rock 'n' Roll Hall of Fame.

Brian Wilson, as writer and producer, singer and musician, is still a driving force behind The Beach Boys, but younger brother Dennis is no longer with them, having drowned while intoxicated off the coast of California in 1983. Brother Carl Wilson, cousin Mike Love, Al Jardine and Bruce Johnston are still with the band and can be seen regularly on cable television's music video stations—another example of The Beach Boys' staying power. While many social and music critics first considered rock and roll evil, promiscuous, lascivious, etc., etc., The Beach Boys, with timeless songs of escapism via the automobile and the sun, via the beach and its bikini-clad denizens, have become, well, to put it bluntly, the rock and roll establishment.

Recording theme songs for such mainstream films as *Cocktail* and *Police Academy IV* have helped keep The Beach Boys in the public eye, as have two national television specials, *The Beach Boys 15th Anniversary Special* (1976) and *The Beach Boys... Twenty-Five Years Together* (1987). Although the members no longer have the youthful appearance of teenagers blowing off classes to catch some waves—rather, they now appear as many men in their late forties do, with slightly balding heads and somewhat protuding paunches—their popularity seems to encompass both people of their own generation and those growing up today. When former National Interior Secretary James Watt banned them from the 1983 Fourth of July celebration at the Washington Monument, the outcry from all age groups was such that then-President Ronald Reagan invited the band to perform at the White House itself.

That Watt believed The Beach Boys attracted the "wrong element" was ludicrous: a scan of the crowd at a later Washington Mall concert showed that today's yuppies, yesterday's hippies, clean-cut college kids, Young Republicans, housewives, lawyers, perhaps even congressional representatives, were all there rockin' and rollin' to songs like "Fun, Fun, Fun," "I Get Around," and "Help Me, Rhonda." As The Beach Boys praised American virtues from the stage, and as the crowd ate hot dogs and watermelon while dancing and singing along with the group, it was obvious what the band had become: a staple part of mainstream, middle-class, cultural Americana.

Yet becoming a foundation, as The Beach Boys are in terms of their influence on both America's music and culture—to wit: the "beach blanket" movies of the 1960s; the popularity of the California lifestyle, not only in the United States but across the world as well; a commercial jingle for California oranges; and the emergence of surfing and surf-wear as a lifestyle that has transcended the sport—has its price. The Beach Boys' success may have enabled them to purchase large homes in exclusive neighborhoods, extravagant sports cars, and whatever other trappings of wealth and fame they desired, but it did not isolate or prevent them from undergoing personal traumas similar to the ones suffered by their peers and devotees.

Foremost among these is the story of Brian Wilson, who almost killed himself by ingesting huge amounts of food and a wide variety of drugs. Weighing more than 300 pounds, he was put on a strict diet and regimen of exercise, and placed under twenty-four-hour-a-day supervision to prevent him from drinking, smoking and snorting any more stimulants and narcotics. Out of both necessity and desire, the rest of the band began writing and producing more material and, while they may not all be good friends, they still appear more than capable of recording and performing music as one group, with even the ever-reclusive Brian occasionally joining them on tour.

Although The Beach Boys' star may not shine as brightly as it once did, the fact that they are willing to come together now and then is a testament to their longevity and to the appeal they have for fans of all generations. Ultimately, however, it is a testament to the success and longevity of their music, for that is what brings both them and their fans together.

—Paul David Seldis
Redlands, California
August 15, 1990

INTRODUCTION
To the First Edition

The Beach Boys are still one of the most accomplished and undervalued groups working in rock music today. Their style defies classification, and their distinctive sound and outlook, which began as smooth, polished, surburban high-school surfing music, has grown to the point where, in the group's *Holland* LP (1973), their "California saga" combines the poetry of Robinson Jeffers with the lilting music of Mike Love and Al Jardine. The result is a powerful and convincing tribute to a majestic landscape that has come to symbolize a state of mind. Jeffers' haunting imagery and The Beach Boys' melodious sound provide a feeling of liberation possible only at the edge of a culture that has stubbornly resisted encroachment from the inert materialism that marks much of contemporary society.

Beginning in the early 1960s, and continuing to the present, the harmonies, lyrics, and melodies of The Beach Boys have reflected many important aspects of American civilization. By listening to the albums they made during that period, one can follow more than a decade of tension and upheaval embodied in popular music. The Beach Boys differ from most other writers and musicians of rock music in their focus on the personal problems and feelings of the ordinary man. And while they did take note of the political and social protests so prevalent during the late 1960s, they always returned in the end to the same basic concerns; in this respect, their vision has been remarkably consistent through fifteen years of playing and recording. The Beach Boys have generally represented a white, middle-class point-of-view, a comforting and reasonable representation of the open, generous, life-enhancing spirit of America.

Exuberance has always been their trademark. They obviously liked what they were singing about, whether it was surf, cars, or girls. Their joyous picture of living transformed the Southern California landscape from just another place on the map into a state of mind, a way of existing. They celebrated not just a land- or beach-scape, but a new cultural lifestyle. Before the advent of The Beatles, The Beach Boys epitomized the idea of a separate "youth culture."

They were equally important for their music. They were among the first rock musicians to produce their own records and emphasize the importance of studio sound. From the beginnings of their career, The Beach Boys exemplified the feelings of those adults who were made uncomfortable by either the appearance or mannerisms of the early performers of rock 'n' roll. At the beginning of the era, in 1955, Bill Haley and The Comets clowned around on stage and screen, the saxophone player doing all sorts of gymnastic feats while honking madly away, the string bassist climbing aboard his instrument while plucking out the rhythm, and so forth. Perhaps Haley's musicians were only imitating the Black rhythm-and-blues performers, but they must have seemed like maniacal showmen to many other whites, trying to arouse the innocent teenage audiences to heaven-knows-what. "Rock Around the Clock" suddenly shot The Comets into international prominence. To tone down the song's growing notoriety (probably the result of its association with the film *The Blackboard Jungle*, where, as the movie begins, the song blasts out from behind the titles; the teenage theater audience at that time often erupted spontaneously into dancing in the aisles), The Comets may have attempted to dramatize the fun aspect of their newly discovered musical style. Their "funning around" could have also have been a deliberate strategy aimed at suggesting that their music was itself mostly harmless nonsense. Titles like "See You Later, Alligator," "Crazy, Man, Crazy," and "Skinny Minny" probably made no sense whatever to white, literate, straight adults, no matter what they might have meant to blues musicians or fans.

Strangely enough, little criticism was aimed at the words of "Rock Around the Clock." Since the term "rock 'n' roll" derived from the blues tradition, where it referred to sexual intercourse, "rocking" around the clock should have raised danger signals among the conservative poulation of middle-class America. Such was not the case. In many songs, however, the lyrics were deliberately softened by the performers to lessen their impact; Bill Haley, for example, made significant changes in his version of Joe Turner's "Shake, Rattle, and Roll."[1] Turner and his song belonged to the tradition of the "Blues Shouter"; it's not surprising, then, that he bids his woman to get herself up out of bed. Haley, a white musician from a country-western background, deletes that potentially troublesome scene by suggesting that she busy herself instead with breakfast; bed isn't even mentioned. Even the slightest hint of indecency was completely expurgated.

Even Haley wasn't prepared for the enormous response his music received from teenage audiences. They swarmed his performances, and exploded into frenetic dancing wherever his band appeared. But where Haley backed away from any possible sexual connotations, other performers, especially Elvis Presley, relished it. "Elvis the Pelvis," as he soon came to be known, aimed his pitch squarely at the female adolescent fan. His success was astonishing. But even Presley was forced to tone down his act when he appeared on national television; the producers of "The Steve Allen Show" deliberately stripped him of any possibility of making unauthorized movements on the program.[2] By dressing him in formal clothing for one song, forcing him to remain frozen in one position, and placing him in a comedy skit, they made quite certain that no one anywhere could possibly be offended by the young star. Elvis' image was even more sanitized when he went into films, and after he was drafted into the army, nothing else remained of the amiable rebel except his natural charm. The young girls still followed him everywhere he went, but he no longer represented a threat to their parents. It took some time before the culture at large learned to accept Elvis and the emotional response of his fans, and what that represented.

Early rock 'n' roll soon became identified with electrically amplified guitars (an identification that unfortunately persists to this day), and the guitar continued to be favored by most groups working in the late 1950s and early 1960s. Like The Beatles, The Beach Boys began their career with guitars, drums, and other stringed instruments. As they matured, both groups added pianos and other keyboard instruments, and then expanded further into more exotic kinds of playing equipment. Even at the beginning, The Beach Boys strove for a fluid and harmonius sound in their music, and although they developed more complicated textures in their later work, the basic effect was the same. Carl Wilson's lead guitar became surrounded by a sumptuous, smooth combination of soft falsetto voices, harp arpeggios, modulated organ runs and chords, and anything else that was needed to create the beautiful sounds imagined by brother Brian.

Other performers stressed more than their music, however, and Jerry Lee Lewis, another popular star of the fifties, created a rebellious image in quite another way. With his frenetic foot-stomping-on-the-keyboard style, and his obvious disregard of the middle-class reverence for fine furniture and everything it symbolized, he insulted some people even more than Presley did. Although the blond rocker delighted audiences with his playing and singing, his basic appeal was more visceral, as can be seen from some of his song titles ("Great Balls of Fire," "Whole Lot of Shakin' Goin' On," e.g.). Undeniably a great showman, he was capable of inspiring terrific amounts of frenzy in his crowds. But his marriage to a 14-year-old second cousin led not only to his exclusion from the British rock 'n' roll scene, but also contributed greatly to his decline in this country.

The most frenetic performer of all, Little Richard, could be ignored by the guardians of good taste as some sort of freak, since he happened to have black skin. Rock 'n' roll music was basically a white product, so Little Richard had to be the result of the blues tradition, and even respectable Blacks knew the blues was the devil's music. In the mid-1950s, Black culture in general was ignored by the white middle class; Little Richard's hooting and chord-pounding piano style could be regarded as just so much more garbage. In those days, the only Black vocalists who attracted a white audience were adult pop crooners who sounded more like Bing Crosby than any blues singer. What bothered their WASP patrons was the fact that their children didn't seem interested in the same kind of music, and instead were buying the records of more raunchy performers, and dancing to a different sort of beat.

Chuck Berry sang specifically for the younger generation and, through his popularity, proved that a huge audience lay there waiting to be tapped. A flood of solo performers and groups, who also reflected problems of their teen-age fans, followed in his wake. His influence is clearly evident in two hits, "School Day," and "No Money Down," which were directly echoed by The Coasters' "Yakety Yak" and The Silhouettes' "Get a Job." At the end of the decade, however, Berry was in jail, Elvis had been toned down in a series of mediocre, money-making films, and the extraordinarily influential Buddy Holly had been killed in an airplane crash.

Thus, by the first years of the 1960s, rock 'n' roll had become a formula-ridden product, redeemed only occasionally by the inventiveness of Phil Spector and his series of girl singing groups. During this period, popular music in America had lost many of the original connections to the traditions that had created the new sound of the previous decade. Instead, a small number of thoroughly professional composers had begun to mine, not the blues or country traditions, but the Broadway and Tin Pan Alley background of the great American songwriters.

The few who survived this era belonged to the latter tradition; singers and composers like Carol King, Paul Anka, and Neil Sedaka had never been more popular. Elvis Presley managed to make the transition from social rebel to the establishment. Other, less adaptable performers either retreated into traditional genre (Jerry Lee Lewis went back into country music), or vanished altogether (Little Richard and Chuck Berry appear infrequently today). The extension of Tin Pan Alley conventions succeeded in blending together a new kind of American popular music, undercutting the rock movement and sapping its vitality, leaving it once again to the experimenters.

Before this trend was firmly established, it was abruptly transformed into a golden age of rock when new stars arose in England and California. The story of how the British groups, led by The Beatles and The Rolling Stones, conquered American pop music is well-known. California's contribution is not as clear. Only a small part of that history can be related here, but The Beach Boys are utterly central to what happened, and their place in the development of the form will become more evident as we talk about their music.

Before proceeding further, however, some mention should be made of popular dancing in the early sixties.[3] Beginning about 1960, the twist swept the adolescent crowd, and rapidly pushed out all other forms of dancing. Then a strange thing happened: the musical center-of-gravity suddenly shifted, and the adult audience began appropriating their children's style of dancing. And with that, of course, came the music associated with the form. The crooners gradually sold fewer records, and dance-oriented songs took over the market. Then, as now, dance music needed a strong beat to be successful. At the same time, the sound could not be so harsh as to assault the eardrums of its listeners. Many artists tried to find a combination that could provide enough beat, tension, and interest to capitalize on the increasing popularity of rock 'n' roll music as a dance form. In Detroit, for example, Motown built on Phil Spector's musical ideas, and hit its stride in the mid-1960s. Yet the center of this creative upheaval was Southern California, where local groups were developing a unique style of music that would soon sweep the country, and continue to influence rock music until today. Only there was popular music sufficiently removed from the other traditional influences (Tin Pan Alley, Blues, Country-Western) to strike out on its own. And the best of these groups was The Beach Boys.

I.
"SURFIN'" TO *ALL SUMMER LONG* (1962-1964)

Although The Beach Boys were first regarded as just another Southern California rock 'n' roll group specializing in surfing music, they were able to outgrow that simplistic image through their considerable musical abilitites. Indeed, their surfing image originated almost accidentally. In their first album, only two songs relating to the sport appeared: "Surfin'" and "Surfin' Safari." The success of these two hits prompted the group to mold itself into the role that had been created for it by its audience. Since the world seemed to require a healthy, outdoorsy, surfing image, The Beach Boys supplied the product demanded by their fans. It's to their credit that they were able to live up to the expectations of their audience, and then transcend such a narrow identification by growing in their music, and taking their following with them.

In the early 1960s, hundreds of small rock 'n' roll groups sprang up overnight, and quickly gathered local patronage of varying sizes; the challenge each had to face was to expand their musical horizons while simultaneously increasing their audience. Most of these bands failed within a relatively short period of time, either because their talents were insufficient to carry them beyond a certain plateau of development, or because internal dissensions within the group, usually caused by personality clashes or the pressures of success, destroyed the atmosphere necessary for the creation of good music. In the history of American rock, The Beach Boys have had the longest life as an integral group; during the course of more than sixteen years, they've managed to weather the many changes in fads and fashions, and still have retained their original followers in Southern California, while building a world-wide audience rivaled in numbers only by fans of The Beatles. Unlike the latter, however, The Beach Boys are still performing as a group, and show no signs of the animosities which plagued Liverpool's Fab Four.

The Beach Boys are more than just another group of high school surfers singing their way into maturity. Rather, they represent a distinctive kind of lifestyle, a Southern California pastoral. In their world, sand- and sea-scape replace the traditional country ideas; the sounds of the surf and the sea drown out the raucous noise of the city. Although their creation may look superficially real to the outside observer, it actually represents a make-believe world unexperienced by the vast majority of their teenage followers. The values of this mythical world are exactly those that describe The Beach Boys' own singing style: cool and colorful, and above all, comfortable. The young adolescent's fancies and fantasies have been transposed into vibrant sound.

To many critics of the time, The Beach Boys looked and sounded hopelessly superficial. It could be argued that such superficiality was all the group was ever capable of; but this surface quality in their music was less of a limitation than might be imagined, and may instead have been the result of a conscious realization that their abilitites had certain creative boundaries beyond which it was not wise to go. Learning to operate freely within one's limits is the first sign of professionalism in the arts.

Their early songs deliberately avoided the richer kinds of experience that filled the records of Chuck Berry in the late 1950s, of rhythm and blues singers Chester Burnett and McKinley Morganfield (known more popularly as Howling Wolf and Muddy Waters, respectively) in the early 1960s, and blues folksinger Bob Dylan. They also refused to compete with the likes of Ray Charles, or the other innovators who were mixing together various styles of popular musical traditions to make the "new sound." Instead, under the leadership of Brian Wilson, they picked their songs carefully, and created a unique style that was perfectly suited to their subject matter, a sound that merged the harmonies and rhythms heard frequently and clearly in white music.

The content of their early music often seemed as superficial as the form in which it was packaged. But this apparent liability often worked in their favor, due largely to the genre in which they worked. The classic pastoral, literally defined, refers specifically to a certain kind of bucolic literature originally composed by Greek poets in the third century B.C.[4] The genre was a popular form in ancient times, and again became widespread during the late Middle Ages. Throughout the Renaissance, pastoral themes appeared widely in the work of the greatest poets and dramatists of the time. Dante, Cervantes, Shakespeare, and Milton all wrote pastorals during the course of their careers. As the pastoral developed, it gradually became more complex. By the time it first appeared in American thought and letters, it had grown into a multifaceted literature able to express the inherent paradoxes in life while still retaining its basic simplicity.[5]

The primary premise of the genre is that everything can be rendered in terms of country scenes or settings. Pastoral innocence, a concept essential to its philosophy, may be expressed either in psychological or religious terms. In either case, the idea is the same: city life is utterly corrupt and corrupting, while the country existence is necessarily wholesome and morally edifying. Those born innocent must guard themselves at all times against the corrupting influences of the outside world, lest they be overwhelmed by forces beyond their control, and swept into the cesspools of society. The influence of the pastoral remains strong even today, as we can see in various cigarette commercials, popular literature (the modern gothic), and the modern idea of the vacation retreat, which spirits us away from the everyday world to a nostalgic, sentimental, bucolic paradise where worries are swept aside by the cool country breezes. The pastoral celebrates country life over city existence, rest over work, peace instead of cares. Life, it says, is a time of renewal, and each day is a new rebirth. Rather than imitate nature, it reembodies it in a fantasy creation flavored with realistic details.

Intentionally or not, The Beach Boys reworked the pastoral theme to capitalize on the idea of Southern California as the new pastoral paradise. By making California a place where young people wanted to be, the group rapidly outgrew its local audience, and was soon hitting the national charts. To fans outside the state, the place names celebrated in a song like "Surfin' U.S.A." had the exotic ring of far-off Xanadu. No less exotic was the sport celebrated by inhabitants of this strange and lovely land. You could ride along in films or on TV, but without an ocean nearby, the best surfing trip available was the crest of your own imagination. California was a gleaming wonderland of eternal sunshine, where the beaches were warm all year round, the girls smiling and friendly and a little bit silly, and the wild waves just waiting for someone to master them.

As might be expected, the pastoral form has its favorite season. To the Greek and Latin poets who first developed it, spring and summer are the favored times of the gods. To The Beach Boys, "Summer

Means Fun," (to borrow the title of Jan and Dean's 1966 recording). School's out, and it's time to let go, all day, and all night, long. The Beach Boys' preoccupation with the season (it would be unkind to label it an obsession) is a natural reflection of their youth at the time the group was formed. In 1962, when they recorded and released their first album, they were scarcely out of high school—Mike Love, the oldest of the group, had just turned twenty-one. And they looked the part they played: youthful, hedonistic surfers who cared only for surf, sun, cars, and girls, not necessarily in that order (but almost). The visual rhetoric of their early record covers, which feature sea, sand and surfboard, helped reinforce this image, and gave the impression that all of their songs were concerned with the sport. Of course, this was not really true. Brian Wilson, the composer, with Mike Love, of their first single, "Surfin'," had never surfed himself; despite this, he was able to convince the surfing crowd and hordes of outside followers that this song, and those that followed, "were written," as one record producer put it, "by someone who was out there hanging ten."[6] The entire surfing culture was mythologized by The Beach Boys.

"Surfin'" was released on the Candix label, with a nonsurfing song, "Luau" (not composed by the group), on the B side. This first record was followed by another pair of songs, one of which, "Judy," was also written by Wilson, although neither of the compositions dealt with the surfing culture. When their first single hit was rerecorded by Capitol Records for the group's first album, *Surfin' Safari* (November 1962), none of the other pre-Capitol songs were included. "Surfin'" suggests some of the culture behind the sport: the surfer needs his radio, girl, and even his special dance, the "Surfer Stomp," to complete his day. Thus, the beach mystique is already being developed.

"Surfin' Safari," the title hit of their first album, carries the process one step further. For the first time, we hear some of the more affectionate phrases in the surfer's language. Girls are honeys, and the vehicles you use to take them and your boards to the beach are woodies (paneled station wagons); and, of course, all of you dress in well-worn blue jeans. We are also given a short geography lesson to lead us around the unfamiliar surfing territory; names like Malibu and Doheny must have sounded strange to anyone outside of Southern California, but they would soon be repeated often enough to become familiar labels country-wide within a year or two.

Also included in the album is "Moon Dawg," a surfing instrumental not composed by The Beach Boys. This particular selection is typical of what surfing music was like before The Beach Boys began to develop their mellow and energetic sound. Like most of its kind, "Moon Dawg" is characterized by a loud, twanging lead guiter, and a rapid, almost raunchy beat; the sound has been altered by an echo chamber. This kind of song rapidly disapeared after The Beach Boys began playing; their wide influence soon became evident as other California groups began imitating their style, and the older music just faded away. The final number in the *Surfin' Safari* album, "The Shift," emphasizes another important element in teenage music and culture—clothes. The song celebrates the soft eroticism of a surfer-girl who really turns the singer on when she wears that certain kind of dress.

While all of these pieces were more or less popular, the song that really broke the group out of its regional mold was "Surfin' U.S.A.," which appeared in March 1963, less than a year after their first local release. By using the music of Chuck Berry's 1958 rocker, "Sweet Little Sixteen," and adding the words and organ of Brian Wilson, the mild falsetto harmonies of The Four Freshmen, and an infectious energy all their own, The Beach Boys created in their audience a powerful urge to pick up a board, head for the ocean, and live out a surfing dream. This was their best performance to that time; within weeks after the record was released, they had a national reputation. I've been told by college students from those days that one would often see cars in the midwest with surf boards bolted to the tops of their roofs; it didn't seem to matter that they were a thousand miles from the nearest ocean—the important thing was just to have the board.

The pastoral imperative of the California lifestyle reached new heights in this song. The concept of an entire generation of teenagers leaving the humdrum environment of school to escape into the surf is a gigantic and utterly compelling fantasy. And while the entire mood of the piece is hypothetical (Brian's first word is "if"), their imaginary world is constructed in the most desirable terms.

Just in case you had not as yet learned what to wear or how to look, Brian supplies the necessary information: long, almost knee-length cut-off denims; rubber-bottomed huarache sandals; blond hair for both sexes, bleached either by the sun or other means. As in the earlier songs, another map is provided: Del Mar, the Ventura County line, Doheny, San Onofre, Redondo Beach, L.A.

The words at the end of the song clearly pinpoint the group's intended audience: teenagers out on their summer vacation. Also, the scope of the song is unmistakable: literally everyone has gone surfing. Once again the chorus is sung in softened falsetto harmonies.

      Wilson adds an insistent and emphatic choral back-beat to the piece by having falsetto voices repeat a phrase behind the safari's itinerary, which itself is a direct quote from surfing language: a surfer's position relative to an incoming wave is described as being either "inside" or "outside," depending upon which way the curl is breaking. Hence, the more you hear the song, the more familiar you become with the specialized jargon of the sport. The song still makes sense whether you catch the special significance of the phrase or miss it completely; it was this kind of added touch that separated The Beach Boys from their numerous imitators. While perhaps insignificant in itself, it does provide a musical and verbal emphasis that enhances the song's exuberance, and reveals Brian's inventiveness. One must remember that The Beatles had not yet conquered America, and most of white rock 'n' roll groups made their respective ways into the charts by imitating black music. The Beach Boys were one of the few groups prior to The Beatles that developed a sound sufficiently distinct from their competitors to set them apart in a class by themselves. "Surfin' U.S.A." reveals Brian Wilson's fertility as a composer and arranger.

      The next two Beach Boys' albums were released in March 1963; curiously, however, the surfing element figures in neither of them. Instead, the emphasis shifts to car songs. For some unexplained reason, the first of these pieces, "409," which had appeared both on their first single record and their first LP, is repeated in what is often called their third album, *Shut Down*. Only two of the songs on this record are by The Beach Boys, however. The "409" in the title refers to a particular kind of car, and, more specifically, to the horsepower of a Chevy V-8 sedan that had been produced as General Motors' answer to Ford's 406 and the legendary Super-Stock Dodge. It was a huge engine for the size of the car, and it became so popular with a certain adolescent crowd that a separate market for 409 tags sprang up overnight. Now it was possible to own a less expensive car that could compete in acceleration (more often at traffic-light intersections than in official drag races) with the standard-size Chevrolets. And if your car didn't actually have the engine, you could at least boast that it did by applying the 409 tags to both sides of the fender just above the bumper.

      The adolescent competitiveness in these songs is a reflection of the harsh intrusion of mechanized civilization into the pastoral world of surf and turf. The ugly noise of roaring mufflers drowns out the sound of the waves, the exhaust smoke pollutes the air, and the resulting haze lingers long afterward over the beach. By turning their attention to the car craze, The Beach Boys are merely bringing up-to-date the fascinating struggle between nature and machine that has marked so much of American culture. Of course, car songs were no novelty in rock 'n' roll music by 1963.[7] As early as 1955, Chuck Berry was singing about "Mabellene," the V-8 Ford that out-raced a Cadillac. Berry's song expresses more about cars than anything The Beach Boys would sing. You were never quite sure whether Berry was just describing his car, or mourning the loss of his girl, who had left him for the Cadillac man, or both. To a Black from the inner city, cars and girls can become one and the same. But to a white, middle-class surfer, the world is wider and brighter, and includes something more than just his wheels and his girl.

In their exploration of the car culture, The Beach Boys strike a basically optimistic note. Although the machine has invaded their pastoral world, their imagery is less aggressive and threatening than complementary. Hence, in their fifth LP, *Little Deuce Coupe* (October 1963), the song titles are flattering: the car is described as a "Custom Machine," and the girl is a "Car Crazy Cutie" who rides in a "Cherry, Cherry Coupe." The word "cherry" in this context doesn't refer to color, but to something particularly superior or refined. Instead of ruining their pastoral vision, the car now makes it possible. For, just as there is a natural geographical association between surfing and the Southern California region, there also exists an equally natural sociological association between surfing and automobiles in that part of the country. Without any means of public transportation, the car assumes immense importance as the only possible way of getting your board to the ocean. Further, the car makes possible a temporary escape from the confining clutches of high school, college, home, family, and job, if only for one day. For that short period of time, you could assume a lifestyle unruffled by any concerns plaguing the real world. Thus, the car became both a symbol of independence and freedom, and the very means by which to assert it. By suggesting the harmony that can be established between the machine and the pastoral vision of the beach as paradise, The Beach Boys confirmed the naiveté that so markedly delineates their musical vision.

The social possibilities of the car, and the peculiar status associated with a particular model, are clearly heard in one of the group's most popular records, "Fun, Fun, Fun" (issued as a single in February

1964, and included in the album *Shut Down, Volume 2* a month later). The song begins with another tribute to Chuck Berry, similar to to one paid earlier when Brian Wilson borrowed the melody of "Sweet Little Sixteen" for "Surfin' U.S.A." Following this introduction, we're told about a little girl who uses her set of keys to cruise in her father's T-Bird (Ford Thunderbird) when she should be studying in the library. One wonders whether the mysterious blonde in *American Graffiti* would have ever driven her white Thunderbird in the film if The Beach Boys hadn't written this song.

Another cruising scene highlights "I Get Around" (a single released in May 1964 and included on the *All Summer Long* LP of August 1964). It appears in retrospect that this particular composition was deliberately released just before school vacations were due to begin, for it celebrates in its exuberant style that time of year when freedom from classes gave one the opportunity to explore new territories, and avoid cruising the old familiar ground or strip (the street where adolescents slowly drove their cars up and down, looking for friends and dates).

Still, the spirit of competition remains basic to the car scene, as is evident in the popularity of "409," which was one of the most frequently recorded songs the group ever played. "409" captures the excitement of the adrenalin "rush" as the chorus urges the driver to rev up the engine, preparatory to beating out the competition; to be beaten in such a race is to be "Shut Down." The Beach Boys' affection for cars and racing shows up again in "Little Deuce Coupe," (included in the album of the same name), in which they praise a modified 1931 Model-A Ford with as much feeling as one might express for a girl, cataloging in detail her virtues and attributes.

In an album released in September 1963, just a month before *Little Deuce Coupe*, The Beach Boys introduce an archetypal image, the *Surfer Girl*. On the surface, this sounds like their earlier work, but certain refinements in their pastoral creation are evident. The most important change is the new image of the girl herself: She now assumes the classic features associated with the "California girl." Like some species of bird, she is classified, but not described in great detail. We see her as blond, tanned, lean, leggy, unbelievably healthy; her likeness is everywhere, in magazine ads and television comercials (especially for hair-coloring products), and in all the beach party and bikini films of the time. *Surfer Girl* recapitulates sounds heard in the group's earlier music. The falsetto background voices recur in "Catch A Wave," which features a lovely harp arpeggio not usually found in teenage pop records. The next cut on the album, "In My Room," is one of the first introspective pieces performed by The Beach Boys. It celebrates relief instead of activity, a place where there are no parents to hassle with, no chores to be done—in other words, a pastoral retreat. The song expresses the universal human longing for some refuge from the hectic pace of everyday life, and the need of everyone for peaceful solitude. It also suggests a necessary retreat from a culture that seems at times too public, too competitive, too much oriented towards making it big.

Four Beach Boys albums appeared in 1963, and four more were issued in 1964, as the group began moving away from simpler themes to encompass more of the outside world. We hear about "Girls On the Beach" in the album *All Summer Long* (August 1964); the pastoral wish fulfillment is particularly strong in this LP. The ideal here is still oriented toward a male adolescent fantasy, although it seems clear that the viewpoint represents a nostalgic look back at high school innocence and naiveté. For example, one cut of the album deliberately evokes the mid-1950s by referring specifically to Little Richard, Chuck Berry, and Elvis Presley, while the raucously biting saxophone of an earlier rock 'n' roll epoch supplies an instrumental sound uncharacteristic of The Beach Boys. Nostalgia also seems responsible for "Drive In," with its perfectly exact references to the old cars in which the windows become easily fogged up; the advice is never to sneak your friends into your car's trunk. A more contemporary note is supplied by "Don't Back Down," another surfing song. As it happens, this piece represents their farewell to the sport, since they were never to record another original surfing tune.

Their final album of 1964, *Beach Boys in Concert* (October), was also their first recorded concert appearance. Four of the songs included on this record utilize the language of the automobile scene, and confirm the suggestion that their car-culture image is distinctly complementary to their surfing background. The other selections are mixed, although they do clearly indicate two of the group's sources for inspiration. The first number is "Fun, Fun, Fun," which in turn is neatly balanced by the last piece, Chuck Berry's "Johnny B. Goode," the source of the guitar run opening their own song. The Beach Boys also try their own variation of the Four Freshmen's "Graduation Day," and fail to bring it off (the original is doubtlessly more polished). However, it is significant that they allow the comparison to be made by their audience, even if their version almost becomes a parody because of some callow attempts at humor. The use of this material clearly indicates that The Beach Boys by now are secure enough in their own identity as a group to smile upon their origins, and to begin searching around for new musical horizons to conquer.

II.
BEACH BOYS TODAY TO *BEACH BOYS PARTY* (1965)

In early 1965, while recording *The Beach Boys Today!* (released in March 1965), Brian Wilson announced to the rest of the group that he would no longer tour with them. The impact on the others was profound. While Brian remained at home and in the studios, continuing to compose, arrange, produce their records, and generally guide the group, the rest decided to maintain their contacts with the public, and Bruce Johnston was eventually recruited by Mike Love to replace Brian while they were on the road. He was a good choice, and in time would write some of the group's most effective material. Still, it was a difficult time for both Brian and the others, and it is to their credit that they never broke up, or even stopped touring.

Much of the increasing seriousness of their music can be attributed to Brian's own difficulties, but other factors also played their part. The Beach Boys were never ignorant of contemporary developments in rock music, and since much of their early success derived from their ability to adapt contemporary styles to their own inimitable sound, they began experimenting with the music created by the other strong names in pop, including Phil Spector, The Beatles, and Bob Dylan. Thus, while the group was hardly politically oriented in those days, that still didn't stop them from recognizing Dylan's genius or importance, as can be seen in *Beach Boys Party!* (November 1965), where they sing "The Times They Are A-Changin'." Also included on that album are three versions of Lennon-McCartney songs, "I Should Have Known Better," "Tell Me Why" (both from The Beatles' 1964 film *A Hard Day's Night*), and "You've Got to Hide Your Love Away" (from The Beatles' more recent picture *Help!*). An earlier album, *Summer Days (and Summer Nights!!)* (June 1965), include their version of a Phil Spector-Ellie Greenwich-Jeff Barry composition they call "Then He

Kissed Me." On the same record, they imitate Franki Valli and The Four Seasons by singing "You're So Good to Me," and also include an instrumental, "Summer Means New Love," which recalls the title of Percy Faith's "Theme From a Summer Place," an extremely popular tune in early 1960. In duplicating the sound and feel of the older piece, Brian Wilson experiments with a full orchestra, including strings, horns, and reeds.[8] And while he echoes the pop sound of the early sixties, he seems to be feeling his way toward the kind of production number that will prove so typical of his later work. At this stage in their development, the group continues to synthesize both the old and the new, and out of this growing complexity in sound will come the revolution of 1966.

While the changing emphasis in their 1965 records cannot be called a completely new shift, there is much evidence that their music is becoming more expressive as time goes on. This is not unexpected. Brian Wilson by this time is 24 years old, Mike Love is 25, and their concerns are changing as their adolescence fades away. As they matured, The Beach Boys began to expand the number of subjects included in their pastoral world. Writers of traditional pastoral gradually began introducing expressions of disappointed love, especially during the sixteenth and seventeenth centuries; The Beach Boys began exploring similar themes in their song "Wendy" (from the the LP *All Summer Long*, issued in August 1964). In time, the idea of thwarted love will become a theme central to their work, but at this point its appearance is almost disguised. "Wendy" is a rock 'n' roll dance-along number. The words are not happy, and painful lyrics are set off by the use of long pauses separating the opening notes. The initial mood is first overtaken, then obliterated, by a strong dancing tempo from the drums, and the emerging, harmonious vocal line combines with the melody to conquer any obvious sadness. At first, we hear a question asking what has gone wrong. The rest of the piece leads up to the singer accepting the fact she's simply gone off with someone else. Her decision may be hard to live with, but life goes on, and the chorus, which had been reinforcing the pain of her departure with a recurring phrase, accepts Wendy's loss in the last line.

We can hear other examples of deeper experiences and feelings in their first 1965 album, *The Beach Boys Today!* (March). "Good to My Baby" reflects a seriousness little shown even a year before, and "Don't Hurt My Little Sister" reveals concern for someone else's feelings that would have been alien to their earlier work. Perhaps the most eye-opening song from the album is "When I Grow Up," which poses questions about the future.

For the first time, the mood is completely different from another song on the album, "Dance, Dance, Dance," which represents a return to their earlier concerns: listening to the radio, and then an afternoon of dancing, both of which provide alternatives to the mundane existence of school. But for The Beach Boys, school is permanently out, and songs such as these are heard less and less with each new album. Other choices lie ahead, the choices seen in "When I Grow Up," a song which applies not only to the group itself, but also to its audience, which is becoming increasingly sophisticated.

These autographical interrogations had never been heard before in the history of rock music, except possibly in Chuck Berry's old rockers, where he asserts his own understanding of others' predicaments. ("Almost Grown" and "School Day," for example). In more contemporary music, the closest approximation was John Lennon's "Help!" which wasn't released until July 1965. The days of having "Fun, Fun, Fun" are drawing to a close, not just for The Beach Boys, but for American culture as a whole. Rock lyrics, probably due to the considerable influence of Bob Dylan, are beginning to reveal a growing concern with adult problems and situations. Awareness of themselves as something other than party-going, mindless, pleasure-seeking goof-offs is beginning to appear in Beach Boys' lyrics.

Correspondingly, their instrumentation is also growing more complex. In "When I Grow Up," a harpischord, an instrument usually associated with "serious" music, supplies a bite and drive to the song that could have been achieved in no other way; this was before The Beatles began their experimentation with more sophisticated instruments than guitar, drums and piano. Brian Wilson has obviously begun to reach for a quality in sound to duplicate an increasing awareness within himself that is guiding him away from the naive lushness of sentimental pop music, and into a broad range of musical experience. The Beach Boys will never again be satisfied to rely on superficial nostalgia evoked by a simplistic mesh of strings and harmonies.

In the history of rock music, 1965 is a year of transition. The widespread changes that affected all of the groups who were able to make the switch can clearly be heard in *The Beach Boys Today* album (November). "Help Me, Rhonda," from that LP, is deceptive in many respects. Outwardly a dance song, it also suggests pain: love affairs don't last forever. The lyrics plead for help, although the song is itself upbeat. The conclusion seems to be that if one can create music out of feeling, that feeling can't be all bad. The writing and playing of the song is itself a way to work through the disappointment; and if the piece is good enough, perhaps the Rhonda addressed in the lyrics will accept an invitation to dance to the composition.

By this time in their career, The Beach Boys have an international following, and their incessant touring has obviously added a new dimension to their music. Songs like "The Girl from New York City," "Salt Lake City," and "California Girls" (all from *Summer Days (and Summer Nights!!)*, released in June 1965) take particular note of their travels, getting away from the regionalism so strongly evident in their early work. The pastoral sense hasn't completely faded, however; "Summer Means New Love" and the title song both deal with familiar themes. Also, for the first time we see in this LP a touch of humor never before used. In the song "I'm Bugged At My Old Man," the evil father has cut his son's long hair in his sleep, tacked boards over his windows, sold his surfboards, and ultimately caused his suspension from school. It's hard to believe the piece means anything in particular, but it does foreshadow more of the same, in songs like "Vegetables," "I'd Love Just Once to See You," and "She's Goin' Bald."

The comical facet of their music is also evident in *Beach Boys Party!*. The spontaneity of this record, its liveliness and good humor, make it stand out in a vintage year. Although it was put together in the usual studio setting, it gives the appearance of a live performance, an off-the-wall, spur-of-the-moment creation in which the group simply played and sang whatever came into their heads. Under the guise of a loose session, The Beach Boys are free to experiment with style and sounds never before used by them. They range over a wide variety of materials, old and new, familiar and strange, stretching their capabilities, and obviously striving to increase their musical powers. The intention: Here we are, this is who we are (for now), and even we don't know where we'll be next time around. A turning point has now been reached, and Brian suggests that it's time for their fans to listen and take stock; great things are in the works.

III.
PET SOUNDS TO *HOLLAND* (1966-1973)

Two important factors must be taken into consideration when examining the work of The Beach Boys following 1965. First, the rock music business had become more competitive than ever before, as musicians, composers, and writers scrambled madly for a limited audience. Too many groups existed for the public to support, and the necessary attrition that resulted left many promising young players and singers without an audience, or at least doing something else besides performing. On the other hand, the few groups that made it to the top suddenly found themselves showered with unimaginable riches practically overnight, and pursued by avid fans to the farthest corners of their private lives. The pressures of success, and the resulting ego problems that often came with them, destroyed as many groups as it helped.

Still, the mid-1960s seem in retrospect a golden age of popular music. Groups like The Beatles, The Rolling Stones, Jefferson Airplane, The Doors, Buffalo Springfield, The Mamas and the Papas, Simon and Garfunkel, and individual performers like Bob Dylan and Harry Nilsson, were all writing, recording, and creating incredibly good music during this period. This list ignores the growing interest in American and English blues, experiments in "country-rock" (by The Byrds, for example, who were mainly influenced by Gram Parsons, one of the founders of The Flying Burrito Brothers), and the developing phenomenon of "super groups" (e.g., Cream; Crosby, Stills, Nash [& Young]). For sheer excitement and real talent, it was a period unmatched in the history of American and English music.

The record industry had been reshaped in the late fifties and sixties as the age of the buying public shifted from the adult to the adolescent level. Sales volume jumped enormously. The change in musical tastes reflected the efforts of society to transform and reform itself. But where the music succeeded, for a short time anyway, in becoming experimental and even challenging to the buying public, society as a whole backed off from any radical changes, and seemed to settle into more rigid behavior resulting in widespread disenchantment and disappointment. By the end of the decade, what promise there was had dissipated.

Another factor in understanding the work of The Beach Boys after the mid-sixties relates once again to the pastoral form and its antecedents. Outwardly, the pastoral vision seems confined to the external world: implicit in its outlook, however, is the assumption that the cheerful order of things necessarily reflects an inner serenity that is also peaceful, happy, and innocent. Over a period of time, some pastoral poets realized that this mythological picture of harmony and order did not really approximate the way things were, that the pastoral paradise was an oasis in the middle of a harsh desert, or a garden surrounded by a savage wilderness. Similarly, internal serenity can easily be upset by the many violent passions raging outside; to examine this peace of mind, and regain it whenever it has been lost, the pastoral must turn inward to the self. Introspection can result from curiosity, religious needs, or a search for pleasure. The Beach Boys demonstrated all three responses in their next few albums.

Six months passed between the release of *Beach Boys Party* and their first album of 1966, *Pet Sounds* (May). But the result was well worth the wait, and the album was not only the finest record yet produced by the group, but it was also one of the truly influential releases in the history of rock music. It still ranks as one of their two or three finest performances. *Pet Sounds* was the first "concept album" in rock, anticipating The Beatles' *Sergeant Pepper's Lonely Hearts Club Band* by a full year. Such headlines are often irrelevant; what does matter is the merit of an album, whether it makes a place for itself both in terms of audience and with other musicians. On both these counts, this record remains, a decade later, a superb innovation in sound, and an extraordinary accomplishment in American popular music.

The album hangs together more coherently than is usually noted by critics. It seems clear that Brian Wilson, who wrote all the music and produced the record, is extending his own prodigious grasp of studio technique, begun scarcely three years earlier. Layer upon layer of strings, keyboard instruments, horns, reeds, striking percussive sounds, and background harmonies from voices laid on over several tracks, create a sound texture more lush, but at the same time more complex, than anything yet heard in rock music. Against this astonishing background, the deceptively simple lyrics, most written by Tony Asher, are clearly sung, and quite easily heard. Hence, a surprising amount of tension is created merely by this juxtaposition of lyrical simplicity and musical complexity, and the result is the most intricate and exciting sound prior to The Beatles' albums *Revolver* and *Sergeant Pepper*.

Pet Sounds is less a headlong leap into unexplored territory than a natural step forward from the group's earlier work. All the sounds we heard before are present here, but in more developed form. The group is exploring at greater depth sentiments that had already been declared. However, everything has been unified in a series of separate, yet connected, movements that focus specifically upon the problems of maturation. Thus, where some groups of the time were celebrating new levels of consciousness achieved through the use of various drugs, religions, or philosophical ideas, The Beach Boys continued to focus upon the more immediate problems of personal relationships. The hedonistic surfers who allegedly never grew up have achieved a sensitivity to human feelings and emotions that few of the trendier rock groups bothered to cultivate; and rather than ignore the problems of living, or bypass them for some esoteric philosophical system, or eccentric and self-indulgent solutions, The Beach Boys decided to meet squarely the dilemma of being vulnerable human beings at a time when so much of life was in turmoil around them.

Pet Sounds tells the story of a love affair, from its beginning in hopeful optimism to the tragedy of separation after things fall apart. There's no real plot to the tale, only a series of separate episodes strung together like motion-picture frames that have been disconnected from the complete narrative. We hear the reactions, the frustrations, the hesitant, tentative gestures of the disappointed lover as he wanders through the ruins of a deteriorating relationship. "Wouldn't It Be Nice" suggests the adolescent, as he naively dreams about love and marriage. This is romantic fantasy at its most optimistic. The lyrics describe a pastoral paradise. But something must be wrong, because all they ever do is talk about it. Perhaps they are too young to marry, like many adolescents; but certainly they are not too young to love, or to suffer from unrequited love.

The second song, "You Still Believe in Me," begins to instill complications in the music through various percussive instruments and horns combined with multiple layers of vocal sound. We hear suggestions in the music that the boy is ineffectual, that his anxiety needs relief. Then, in the next three pieces, the sense of passivity seems to increase, until it borders on depression. The affair is not going well. The thickly textured strings, played against guitar and drums, together with the piercing percussion instruments behind the multi-layered vocals, increase the tensions between what the young man desires and what he actually feels. He tries to defend himself, explain himself to his love, but he fails. His mood is evident in the title of the fifth song, "I'm Waiting for the Day." That is, he passively is waiting for her to decide. The initiative no longer belongs to him, if it ever did.

The next to last cut on the first side is one of two instrumental tracks on the album. The final song, "Sloop John B.," a traditional folksong arranged by Brian Wilson, seems on the surface to be out of place. Having been released two months earlier as a single, and having had some success in that form, it seems almost to stand alone, apart from the album. Actually, however, Wilson has added exactly those sounds to the number to make it the capstone of the first side. The instrumentation behind the vocal line recapitulates all the sounds heard earlier on side one; thus, the folksong helps unify the initial part of the record. Also, the words of the old song imply a good deal more than they otherwise would because of the special context in which they are placed. For example, the line "this is the worst trip I've ever been on" now suggests a response to the love affair itself, as well as the extended metaphor of the "bad trip," borrowed from the drug culture. The irony of these words was probably unintended in older versions of the song, but seems unmistakable as The Beach Boys sing them. The singer continues his lament: he feels "so broke up," and "want(s) to go home" because things are not working out for him. The meaning of this ballad depends in large part upon the audience realizing the implications of the old song's significance in context. Brian has reworked a familiar folksong to suggest that the present generation grafts new, more relevant ideas onto the obsolete order of things.

Side two of *Pet Sounds* opens with another of the group's best songs. Once again, multiple layers of percussion instruments, bass guitar, and voice merge to support the emphatic beat behind the words of "God Only Knows." The Beach Boys have come a long way since "Wouldn't It Be Nice." The new song not only compliments the girls, but also reveals the lover's dependence on her, laying the responsibility for supporting their continuing relationship directly on the female. Another complex cut is "Here Today," the third number of this side. The title suggests that their close relationship is only temporary. The beginning of a new affair is a glorious time, filled with happiness and light; the singer is recollecting these halcyon days as the relationship degenerates around him. As he laments in the next song's title, "I Just Wasn't Made for These Times," he throws his hands up in despair: the world has defeated him. The second instrumental track follows, in exactly the same position as the one on the first side.

The final song on the album, "Caroline, No," sums up all the unfulfilled expectations left hanging at the end of the affair. It seems to represent one final attempt to retrieve the happy, romantic, pastoral time of youth. The innocence of love is lost forever, and all we can do is wonder where that sunny place went to and lament its passing. The change in feeling is signaled by the girl, who always controlled the relationship; as she grows into a woman, and her appearance alters accordingly, the union comes to an end. But the song is not over. Brian adds an example of what would be called "concrete music," if this were a classical piece. The noise of a railroad train, and the sound of barking dogs, brings the record to an appropriate close. Not only do we hear Wilson's *Pet Sounds*, his favorite musical sonorities, but also the yapping of live pets.

The early pastoral notions of The Beach Boys have now been drowned out by reality. The innocent, uncomplicated life of the surfer has been overtaken by the technology of modern civilization. You can't go on surfing forever. Henceforth, the group will strike out in new directions, as their pastoral visions turn inward, and are replanted in more fertile pastures. The complications of the late 1960s remain unravelled, and The Beach Boys, not surprisingly, reflect the social currents prevalent in that complicated and contradictory era. Their middle-class outlook remains, however. Earlier in the decade, their pastoral music popularized the California dream, associating with it the images of beach, sea, surf, sand, girls, cars, and all the rest. California was the promised land of America's westward trek. Now, however, other factors were surfacing which threatened to warp that dream into a caricature of itself. Occultism, ecology, fads, drugs, hallucinogens, and cults of all kinds swept middle-class youth, creating the hippie and peace movements, and engineering the mass alienation of an entire generation. The surfer of the early sixties became the flower child of the late sixties. These new concerns of the adolescent world surface in the group's next record, "Good Vibrations" (a single released in October 1966).

Just as *Pet Sounds* remains their best album to date, so is "Good Vibrations" their best single work; indeed, it has been regarded as their masterpiece by many critics. Although the record contains little that has not been heard before, Brian Wilson's love affair with sound finally reaches its peak on this single, which was six months in production. His reach finally catches up to his grasp, for his mastery of technique and sound texture will probably never be surpassed. One must realize that "Good Vibrations" appeared at a time when the psychedelic movement was about to move its center from Hollywood to San Francisco. The new pastoral landscape suddenly being uncovered by the young generation provided a quiet, peaceful, harmonius trip into inner space. The hassles and frustrations of the external world were cast aside, and new visions put in their place. "Good Vibrations" succeeds in suggesting the healthy emanations that should result from psychic tranquility and inner peace. The word "vibrations" had been employed by students of Eastern philosophy and acid-heads for a variety of purposes, but Wilson uses it here to suggest a kind of extrasensory experience. A sensitive person, someone who has been "turned on" to life, can pick up vibrations emanating from people, places, or objects. These waves are perceived as rainbow-colored auras, even when they are invisible to the external eye. Good vibrations elevate, elating the receptor, and filling him with joy. A person with good vibrations is fun to have near. A place with good vibrations is a good place to be. And the lyrics of this song convey exactly these feelings. Behind the words, the studio-controlled sounds of the music enhance the visionary feeling of the number. A theremin wails above, behind, and within the melodic line, giving the ever-present harmonies an almost cosmic dimension. The Beach Boys have subsumed the occult into their music, producing a new hybrid: occult-rock.

The Beach Boys waited over a year before releasing their next album. One single, "Heroes and Villains," did appear in the interim, but it seems to have been overlooked in the aftermath of The Beatle's new LP, *Sergeant Pepper's Lonely Hearts Club Band*. In response to that record, and to others The Beatles had released earlier, rock music in both England and America was evolving away from the type of sound The Beach Boys had popularized. Rock had become a vehicle for political change, or a reflection of an acid trip. Groups like Jefferson Airplane, The Grateful Dead, and dozens of others created a new California sound, and moved the center of creativity from the Los Angeles area north to the San Francisco Bay region. As a result of this change from south to north, The Beach Boys were suddenly left out in the cold. The next work planned by Brian Wilson and his new collaborator, Van

Dyke Parks, was never finished; *Smile* remains one of the great ghost albums in American popular music. Stories still abound concerning its near-legendary contents. Some of the pieces planned for that album do survive in altered form, however, on their next record.

Smiley Smile (September 1967) is a strange album, and it was received by the public with much muttering, and even greater silence. Curiously, nearly everyone praised the first cut, "Heroes and Villains," even though it had been largely ignored as a single release (July 1967)—perhaps because it is a difficult song to understand. Beginning with an ambiguous, quasi-autobiographical opening, it then becomes a kind of love song in a cowboy mode, only to shift abruptly ahead in time with talk of children. Behind the words ranges a kaleidoscope of lightly-textured sound, vocal as will as instrumental, interrupted by harsh, intrusive noises. The total effect is, in some respects, even more beautiful than "Good Vibrations," although the piece does not hold together as well. Nonetheless, Wilson shows a wider range of sound and rhythm than ever before.

The major element in the next track, "Vegetables," is humor. Wilson uses jug sounds, pouring water, and good-natured munching to mock vegetarianism and food fads (at one time Brian was deeply into natural foods). "Fall Breaks and Back to Winter" is an experimental instrumental track that suggests an attempt to alter our perceptions of time, in and out of music. "Wind Chimes," on side two, is another strange piece, evoking what might be a drug-induced state of somnolence. "She's Goin' Bald" reflects a certain nightmarish humor associated with bad drug trips, or "bummers." *Smiley Smile* epitomizes what had happened to rock music by 1967. The days of rock 'n' roll being used primarily for dancing had vanished. Writers and musicians are demanding their audience's attention as they turn their skills to increasingly serious themes. And somewhere along that tortured way, The Beach Boys lost much of their audience to groups like The Beatles, or to individuals like Bob Dylan.

In an effort to regain some of their lost following, The Beach Boys released their next album, *Wild Honey* (December 1967), within a surprisingly short period of time. The title song resembles the number "Gettin' Hungry" on their previous record: both are gutsy rhythm-and-blues pieces written by Brian Wilson and Mike Love. The rest of the album lacks any real unity, even though the first three numbers definitely belong together, representing the group's belated recognition of the Motown sound. The Beach Boys' version of the sound, an adaptation of an older and simpler rhythm and blues to the multiple-layered studio technique that they pioneered, results in an anomalous effort. Only one song in the album truly reflects their direction at this time, the lovely "Country Air." This song recognizes the growing importance of the counter-culture movement that was turning a large number of young people against the ideal of the sophisticated urban life. In pastoral phrases quite unlike any they have used before, The Beach Boys sing about breathing the pure country air, and they go on to praise the basic simplicity of life away from the city. The "easy-listening" strings and gentle texture of the song create an exceptionally simple, but lovely, atmosphere.

Their next album, *Friends* (June 1968), is undistinguished musically, but remains historically important since it marks the appearance of Al Jardine as author or co-author of five songs. Dennis Wilson also makes his initial appearance as a writer, and is credited with four numbers. For the first time, all five of the original Beach Boys collaborate on a song, "Be Here in the Morning." As the title of the record proclaims, they are indeed all friends. Brian seems to have simplified his intentions in this album. His "Busy Doin' Nothin'" is a gem; unpretentious, conversational, wholly without stress. Two of his brother's Dennis' efforts, "Little Bird" and "Be Still," are written in a similar mood, but are more intense. The one major disappointment in *Friends* is the song that reveals, in retrospect, a vital moment in the group's career. "Transcendental Meditation" resulted from their infatuation with the teachings of Maharishi Mahesh Yogi. Unfortunately, the saxophone used in the piece, perhaps meant to suggest the drone of the Indian tambura, sounds instead almost like an old swing sax left over from the 1940s.

The Beach Boys' next album, *20/20* (March 1969), opens with "Do It Again," a number that is almost an old-fashioned rocker. Curiously, The Beach Boys have now played together for so long that some of their earlier songs are undergoing a revival. By this time, the rock 'n' roll revival has been underway for some time and, ever-faithful in reflecting the times, the group immediately picks up the latest popular trend. As with their previous record, Brian Wilson has become somewhat less involved in writing and producing; Bruce Johnston contributes some of the writing and productions, particularly in "The Nearest Faraway Place," as does Dennis Wilson. In fact, this particular record is notorious for the song "Never Learn Not to Love," written by Dennis in collaboration with the infamous cult leader, Charles Manson.[9]   Manson, of course, was later convicted, with some of his "family," for the Tate-LaBianca murders in August of 1969. Dennis was only peripherally involved with the Manson clan, and none of the other members of The Beach Boys were in any way connected with this macabre business.[10]

20/20 also includes a spirited version of "Cotton Fields," "I Went to Sleep," a lovely melody by Brian Wilson along the lines of "Busy Doin' Nothin'," and several lesser pieces. The album is characterized by its wide variety of material, and also by the fact that production of the songs was split up among the various members of the group: Brian did four, Carl another four, and Dennis handled three others. However, Brian continues to be the most inventive of the lot, arranging an a capella choir for his short number, "Our Prayer." Another collaboration with Van Dyke Parks, "Cabinessence," closes the album, and again suggests that their unfinished and unreleased album, *Smile*, was an unfortunate loss to popular music. The song is the most interesting and puzzling piece on the record.

Sunflower (Fall 1970) was their first album produced and distributed by Warner Brothers (the earlier *Smiley Smile* appeared under the Brother label, but Capitol Records had distributed it). Diversity in both songs and styles continues to characterize their work, and the quality of the album remains consistent. The Beach Boys cared too much for a perfect, polished sound ever to allow lapses in production. Indeed, some critics have criticized them for this inherent smoothness, feeling that harsher, more real, more spontaneous music is preferable. The Beach Boys' love for sound of all kinds is evident in the number "Add Some Music to Your Day," wherein they catalog the various kinds of music in the world, and celebrate them all. The spirit of gentle tolerance and acceptance is achieved in both words and melody, as the persistent harmonies and easy-to-follow beat of the harpsichord lead us through the lyrics.

Bruce Johnston contributes "Dierdre," a gentle love song that differs completely from the acid rock and "heavy metal" styles popular at that time. The Beach Boys never ignored popular trends, but, at the same time, they were never afraid to follow their own creative course, picking and choosing what they wanted from the differing styles proliferating around them. At this point in their career, they were particularly interested in transcendental meditation, the education of the spirit, mind, and heart, and interpersonal relationships. "Our Sweet Love" sums up this evocation of incense, flowers, and warmth in a pop-vocal background underscored by cellos. It is almost a recapitulation of their early "romantic" sound, but the "love" in this song is not the sexual kind frustrated in *Pet Sounds,* but the love of a more mature relationship that nurtures the spirit. The record concludes with a response to the ecology movement, "Cool, Cool Water," which is similar to their earlier song, "Country Air" (Brian Wilson and Mike Love wrote both pieces). The idea in both is the same: nature and the things in it are good, and man destroys nature. The pastoral has been renovated in the cause of preserving the Earth; learning to appreciate the natural countryside leads to the reestablishment of harmony within the world and ourselves.

Surf's Up (1971) is one of The Beach Boys' finest achievements. The title is deceptive. The album is definitely not a call to surfers, or even to a nostalgic return to an earlier, more simplistic style. Rather, the record encompasses several topical subjects as it looks back over the entire decade of the 1960s. The first song, "Don't Go Near the Water," is a backward glance at the last song on their previous album. The pastoral world is being destroyed by man himself, as he pollutes the environment. "Long Promised Road" suggests the struggle ahead; the old solution, California as the promised pastoral paradise, will no longer do. The trek westward, celebrated in American myth and song, has reached the edge of the continent, and there is no other place to go. Since we cannot go forward, we must remake what we now have. The serious mood of this piece is relieved by the next cut, "Take a Load Off Your Feet," a humorous treatment of the popular health cults in Southern California. One of the jewels of the album follows: Bruce Johnston's "Disney Girls" (1957) is the California fantasy fulfilled, an evocation in words, sound, and mood of a simpler existence, one epitomized in the smile of a girl transformed into a faithful wife.[11] Few of The Beach Boys' songs celebrate the traditional happy ending; this one suggests that present happiness and a fruitful future can be expressed through a series of sentimental and nostalgic references to the past.

The last cut on side one quickly breaks the mood. "Student Demonstration Time" is the group's response to the many political activists of the time who were urging violence to achieve their ends. The Beach Boys' advice: Cool it! In a clever sort of way, The Beach Boys are pointing to their own limitations. The group has always been cool, often lacking the passion and outward commitment so prized by critics in other rock stars. Side two opens in a different mood. "Feel Flows" is a beautiful song; Carl Wilson's music blends harmoniously with Jack Rieley's lyrics to create a flowing sound that highlights the song's themes. A lovely flute slowly weaves its way through the music amidst a panoply of alliterated vocal glides of "w" sounds—an astonishing eight in the first seven lines. The sense of the lyrics is obscure, but the poetic devices harmonize with the currents of melody and background orchestration to form a unity of flowing feeling. Ultimately, the song suggests that the transcendent or meditative state reveals the reality within us, a reality where everything feels, everything flows, in calm peacefulness. One achieves such perception by cutting through the past, as evoked by memories or present-day frustrations, until one perceives the inner self.

"Looking At Tomorrow (A Welfare Song)" transports us into a world where we can all seek relief. Although out of work, the speaker does not protest, nor does he call for revolution; rather, he remains basically optimistic. The thought and style of the song recalls many old folksongs through the use of an acoustic guitar. The kind of revolution approved by The Beach Boys is celebrated in "A Day in the Life of a Tree," in which one must pierce beneath the surface of things to discover their essence. In this case, our empathy with growing, living plants makes us rebel against the air pollution killing off the trees. Trees are important parts of our world. "Till I Die" is another one of Brian Wilson's remarkable metaphors, realized in words and song. The soul recognizes its oneness with all other existence.

But the best is saved for last. In another marvellous collaboration with Van Dyke Parks, Wilson creates a song of marvelous comlexity in "Surf's Up." Once again, Brian's gorgeous sonorities support a string of images to create a unity of sound. As the music proceeds, its mood changes: a tired decadence overcomes the remembrances in the first part of the song. Self-pity seems to defeat the broken man, but he is revived. Then his direction abruptly changes; he turns around to join the young in spirit. Regeneration in spirit does not come about by forgetting the past; on the contrary, only by immersing oneself in the past can a person develop a new awareness of his inner life. The experiences of youth support the maturity of manhood. *Surf's Up* is a fully developed concept album of the seventies, one of the few advances in sound beyond The Beatles' *Sergeant Pepper* and *Abbey Road*. It stretches one's imagination in sound to encompass ecological and transcendental subjects, and, as such, remains the most ambitious album The Beach Boys have completed.

In terms of their development, the *Holland* LP brings the group full circle. They leave California, the edge of the new world, for Amsterdam, an old-world city facing a different ocean. In this new setting, we hear The Beach Boys return again to the sea in "Sail On, Sailor" and "Steamboat." But the longest piece on the album reveals a more particular concern. From a European setting, they look back at their own land, California, which also borders an ocean; their temporary exile gives them a new perspective on their own country.

The state of mind symbolized in this album approaches that of *Surf's Up*. Peaceful images override the struggle to declare an open desire for tranquility, and a continuity in cosmic harmony rides above and behind the "California Saga." The ocean is a huge encompassing symbol wherein the eternal struggle can complete itself. The group now recognizes America in a new way: their home turf becomes a place to make, perhaps, a new beginning, a spot from which to embark upon an upward turn in the cycle of life.[12]

At the beginning of their career, The Beach Boys were still children, and they acted like children. Now they have become men, and their concerns are those of the adult world. *Holland* represents no new departure for the group. Rather, it gathers together their creative forces, not so much to explore new territory, but to pull their past experiences into a unified whole. But they cannot stand still; at the edge they look back and reassess their music, their country, and themselves.

The *Holland* album remains their most recent original work at this writing (Spring 1976). The Beach Boys have not been inactive, however. A new series of concerts have brought them thousands of new fans while drawing their old friends back once again to live performances. But one wonders how long they can ride the nostalgia wave. Undoubtedly, many listeners in the seventies are discovering forgotten, or even previously unnoticed, value in their 1960s' songs. Still, today's fans certainly include many who would like to hear something more than double albums of repackaged material containing nothing more recent than 1969 numbers. It is true, of course, that there seems to be no commercial reason for the group to get back into the studio. They are probably selling more albums now than at any point in the last five years. But concert successes are not enough, and the interest suggested by sales of their older material indicates that their public is waiting for The Beach Boys to sing out with new songs in the second half of the seventies.

IV.
STILL CRUISIN'
(1976-1990)

The second half of the seventies and the entire decade of the eighties saw The Beach Boys re-issue many of their older hits, briefly foray into the faddish world of disco music and, most importantly, garner their first number one hit nation-wide in twenty-two years, the single "Kokomo" (1989).

While the band did release some new material on LPs such as *The Beach Boys Love You* and the *MIU Album* (Brother/Reprise, 1977 and 1978, respectively), the bulk of their albums were either collections of oldies, such as *Spirit of America* (Capitol, 1975) and *15 Big Ones* (Brother/Reprise, 1976). Although the latter was a compilation of famous, old-time rock 'n' roll hits written by artists such as Phil Spector and Chuck Berry, 1979's *L.A. (Light Album)* is most well-known for it's ten minute-plus disco version of "Here Comes the Night," which originally appeared on 1967's *Wild Honey*. The album did sell more than 400,000 copies, but it also turned off the group's more loyal and purist-oriented fans. Consequently, a look at some of the song titles from *The Beach Boys* (Capitol, 1983) reflects both the overall focus of their musical output during this period and what the bulk of their audience wanted to hear: "Sloop John B.," "Catch A Wave," "409," "Wild Honey," "Why Do Fools Fall In Love?"—all rereleases or remakes of old hits.

Perhaps the most interesting aspect of 1985's *Golden Harmonies* compilation is the cover. Set in a golden frame, it shows a postcard-like picture of "today's" Beach Boys running along the shoreline. Most prominent is Brian, running in the middle of them all, his large, white, untanned stomach thrust forward and bearded head tilted back. He seems to be enjoying himself, as does the rest of the band. Boys will be boys, one supposes, and some never do forget how to frolic, or what got them to where they are today—pastoral, excapist-themed, harmony-based rock 'n' roll.

More recently, The Beach Boys' *Still Cruisin'* album (Capitol, 1989) shows that the group's themes, if not their exact personnel, remain the same. "Kokomo" in particular reflects the pastoral escapism the band has embodied since 1962's "Surfin'." Part of the soundtrack of the hit movie *Cocktail*, the song proved to be The Beach Boys' third number-one single, and their first since "Help Me, Rhonda" twenty-two years earlier. While it no doubt helped that cinema heartthrob Tom Cruise starred in the film and in the accompanying "Kokomo" video, the song's lyrics about getting away to a beachy island are timeless. The rhythmic structure of the verses, along with the mellifluous harmonies and simple rhymes that accompany it, are pure Beach Boys.

The song's use of exotic locations such as Aruba, Jamaica and Montego is especially appealing to today's constantly-moving yuppies. It might be getting away only for a long weekend, or perhaps a week or two, but it is still a temporary escape from the crowded, polluted, life-choking city. It is still packing one's bags, grabbing one's boards, and hitting the beach. In today's fast-paced, short-distanced world, the surfboard might be encased in the baggage compartment of a 747 instead of strapped to the roof of a wood-paneled station wagon, but times change, and so do the modes of traveling to that much-desired pastoral paradise.

The first cut and title track on the album, "Still Cruisin'," could ironically be applied to the group itself, and the fact that, as the song says, the band is after all these years, still cruising. The title phrase is applicable on other levels as well, and one wonders if The Beach Boys are trying to be both playful with their audience and to point a self-aware finger at themselves. Their present-day fans are a mixture of young people and their parents, the former teenagers who now comprise today's upwardly mobile professional working class. In a dual sense, the group is saying, "Look at us. We're still alive and kicking after all we've been through, and so are you." It is an upbeat number that touches not only upon growing older, but also upon that timeless Beach Boys' theme of cruising in your car to get to a sandy and sunny playground. Perhaps because the song and its lyrical simplicity appeals to fans in this three-fold manner, The Beach Boys frequently open their current live performances with this tune. To enjoy it, all you have to do, to paraphrase an automotive command heard in the song, is get in gear.

Similarly, the third and fourth cuts on the LP reflect themes that have always been the group's central focus. Written by Alan Jardine, "Island Girl" is, as the title implies, about a beautiful island girl whom the singer falls in love with. The lyrics and their theme are simple, the singer wants only to live with his fantasy-fullfilling island girl underneath a palm tree near the water. Through her, he wails, he can find eternal happiness, his pastoral paradise on Earth.

"In My Car," composed by Brian Wilson, Wilson's former live-in psychiatrist Eugene Landy, and friend Alexandra Morgan, is a slightly more old-fashioned Beach Boys number, relying on traditional, high-pitched, double-tracked harmonies to describe how great it is to be riding in one's car. The vocals are so whiny and high-pitched that the song has a strong fifties rock 'n' roll sound to it, which, as mentioned ealier, is when cars first became an American symbol of freedom and fun. With a car, no matter the make or the model, life is ripe with endless opportunities for fun, and for escaping the job-demanding city.

Viewed overall, side one of *Still Cruisin'* further illustrates The Beach Boys' historical ability and willingness to incorporate musical sounds and instruments not found in traditional, "pure," guitar-and-drums rock 'n' roll. "Kokomo" uses steel drums and Hawaiianesque strings to elicit a strong, tropical tone (The accompanying promotional copy described the number as "...cooler than a piña colada".), while "Island Girl" combines the group's trademark falsetto background harmonies with more steel drums and a strong, reggae-tinged dance beat. Appropriately, "Somewhere Near Japan" opens with a brief, Asian-toned overture of strings before lapsing into more usual rock 'n' roll, Beach Boys-style music.

If 1973's *Holland* represented the band's venturing eastwards to find their roots, side one of *Still Cruisin'* symbolizes The Beach Boys' full-circle return to the west, to sandy, bikini- and surf-covered beaches, and to the type of music that has always been the band's mainstay—and what makes it so timeless for its fans.

Cognizant of this, side two takes the premise one step further, consisting as it does of remakes of The Surfaris' "Wipe Out," and earlier Beach Boys' hits "I Get Around," "Wouldn't It Be Nice," and "California Girls." The first number, "Wipe Out," is particularly interesting because it was recorded with the rap group Fat Boys, and comes off as a sort of friendly battle-on-recording-tape between the two divergent styles of music. The song, the title of which is taken from surfers' descriptions of what happens when you try to ride a wave and crash instead, begins with The Beach Boys harmonizing in the background, in tune with the pounding drum beat and bass-like lead guitar that has made the song famous (and once very popular with beginning high school garage bands). Suddenly a deep, aggressive voice breaks in, followed by another barking out an updated version of the tune's original lyrics. As the rapper's break into their standard microphone noises, The Beach Boys sing the "wipe out" chorus in their trademark, mellifluous tones. The song comes off as a unique combination of traditional, white rock 'n' roll and modern, street-inspired black rap music. The contrast between the two is even more incongruous when, visually speaking, the two groups are juxtaposed, as they are in the accompanying video—here you have The Beach Boys, white, middle-aged clean-cut, California-born rock 'n' rollers attired in bright, beachy, flower-printed shirts, on stage next to a group of young, Brooklyn-born black musicians clad in dark jeans and shirts, oversized gold chain after gold chain dangling from their necks, extremely large buttocks and hips (ergo, the "Fat Boys" title) bopping up and down.

Still, the song has a certain, ironic and self-parodic appeal, the lyrics having been changed to refer to The Beach Boys as modern-day white rappers, and the surfers who have come west looking for sun, girls and fun are now black, city-dwelling teenagers instead of white college kids from the Midwest. The Beach Boys seem willing to make fun of themselves, and to be aware of their contribution in developing rock 'n' roll. The effect and tone of the song seems to be that every one, black or white, resident of urban or pastoral landscape, rapper or rock 'n' roller, can have fun with their music.

The next cut on side two is "Make It Big," written for the film "Troop Beverly Hills" by Terry Melcher, guitarist Bill House and Mike Love. The existence of the movie must have been the *raison d'être* of this number, for it is a vacuous, airheaded, albeit catchy, song that adds nothing to the group's musical repertoire.

The rest of side two, the aforementioned remakes of three of the band's bigger hits, are well-mixed renditions of these earlier releases, but, as such, add no musical insight into the group's recordings.

However, they do, along with the cuts on side one, provide some glimpse of The Beach Boys future as a recording and performing band. While the group's members may desire to create new material, the ability to be successful at this, and to have the works judged according to their own merit, may not exist. The Beach Boys' past is so big, so famous, so uniquely sounding, that any composition by either the group as a whole or by its individual members will be compared to hits like "Good Vibrations," "Surfin' Safari," and "Help Me, Rhonda." And it is hits like these that The Beach Boys are not only known for, but have also conditioned their fans to desire. As one reviewer wrote of a recent concert:

> Overall, The Beach Boys showed why they have lasted so long despite a lack of successful new material throughout the 80s. Their oldies remain fresh and energizing no matter how many times you hear them and their fans...are more than willing to recognize this.[13]

In light of this, The Beach Boys will more than likely continue to tour and to mix future albums with new, commerically inspired numbers and old, already established, past hits. The themes of both, however, will more than likely stay the same: fast cars, beautiful women, and sun-covered beaches. After all, that is what has made them famous and successful, and that is what the ideal of Southern California pastoral, thanks in large part to The Beach Boys, is all about.

AFTERWORD

In the fourteen years since the publication of *The Beach Boys: Southern California Pastoral*, rock music has undergone changes that few critics would acknowledge as having been predictable. Disco, punk, new wave, and rap have in turn had their impact on the pop music world. Likewise, The Beach Boys have sustained unforeseen shocks that could have erased the group from the contemporary musical environment. To describe and discuss the most important of these (e.g., Brian Wilson's involvement with Eugene Landy, the drowning death of Dennis Wilson) would be, however, to alter severely the focus of this book.

Musically, their significant accomplishments during these years have been almost embarrassingly few. I count them as Brian Wilson's 1988 solo album and the re-release on compact disc of the early Beach Boy albums, especially their magisterial *Pet Sounds*. It looks as if the group has been overtaken by time. But the intrinsic quality of their music, along with the powerful tug of nostalgia, will prevent them and their music from ever being forgotten. Yet generations change, and audiences do not necessarily continue to respond in the same way or to the same material that they used to.

One intriguing example of both continuity and change through generations and gender is provided by the huge success in the spring and summer of 1990 of the vocal group Wilson Phillips. Their debut album spawned exciting music videos, providing hit singles as well as significant album sales. Their interest for me, however, lies in the people who comprise the trio: Carnie and Wendy Wilson are Brian Wilson's daughters, and Chynna Phillips is the only child of The Mamas' and the Papas' John and Michelle Phillips. Two groups that gave such distinctive songs and harmonies to the sixties are heard now in the nineties, but filtered through the voices of their progeny.

Listening to The Beach Boys makes it possible through imagination if not memory to re-experience the bouyant energy that, through gorgeously textured harmonies, suggest what it might feel like to "catch a wave" and be always ready and able to "dance, dance, dance" and have "fun, fun, fun" in their timeless world of the pastoral.

—*Bruce Golden*
California State University
San Bernardino, California
October 15, 1990

AN OVERVIEW OF BEACH BOYS RELEASES

"Surfin'" breaks into the top three of Los Angeles' radio charts, and reaches 75 on *Billboard's* national charts; January 1963.

"Surfin' Safari" spends 17 weeks on the charts, climbing as high as 14; October 1962.

"Surfin' U.S.A." spends 17 weeks on the charts as well, climbing to number 3; "Shut Down" goes to number 13; March 1963.

Surfin' U.S.A. hits the album charts for 78 weeks, topping out at number 2; July 1963.

Surfer Girl and "Surfer Girl" both go to number 7 on the album and single charts, respectively; simultaneously, "Little Deuce Coupe" goes to number 15; 1963.

"Little Deuce Coupe" stays on the charts for 46 weeks, reaching number 4; 1963.

"Be True to Your School" climbs to number 6; 1963.

"Fun, Fun, Fun" occupies the fifth spot on the charts. The Beatles unprecedentally own spots 1-4; March 1964.

"I Get Around" reaches number 1; July 4, 1964.

All Summer Long hits number 4; July 1964.

"When I Grow Up" climbs to number 9; October 1964.

The Beach Boys goes to number 1; "Dance, Dance, Dance" breaks the top ten; December 1964

"Do You Wanna Dance?" reaches number 12; Winter 1965.

"Help Me, Rhonda" stays on the charts for 14 weeks, hitting number 1 and becoming the group's second top-selling single; April 1965.

"California Girls" climbs to number 3; July 1965.

"Barbara Ann" rises to number 2 on American charts; *Beach Boys Party!* reaches number 6, spending six months on the charts; November 1965.

"Caroline, No" rises to number 32; the folk song "Sloop John B." climbs to number 3; March-May 1966.

Pet Sounds stays on the album charts for 39 weeks, rising to number 11 and selling more than 500,000 copies; Summer 1966.

The Best of the Beach Boys goes gold, spending 79 weeks on the charts and reaching as high as number 3; Summer-Fall 1966.

"Good Vibrations" sells more than 700,000 copies its first week out, eventually climbing to number 1 in both England and the United States; Fall-Winter 1966.

"Heroes and Villains," first single released since "Good Vibrations," holds number 12 for two weeks; August-September 1967.

Best of the Beach Boys—Volume 2 stays on the charts for 22 weeks, topping out at number 50; Summer 1967.

Smiley Smile holds the charts for 21 weeks, topping out in the 50s; Fall 1967.

Wild Honey climbs to number 24, spending 15 weeks on the charts; Winter 1967-68.

"Bluebirds Over the Mountain" tops out at number 61; *20/20* receives little fanfare; Winter 1968-69.

Sunflower released on Warner Brothers; a smash in Great Britain, it flops in the United States; August 1969.

Surf's Up climbs to number 29; Summer 1971.

Carl and the Passions—So Tough released with *Pet Sounds*; Winter 1971-72.

Holland spends 26 weeks on the charts, topping out at number 37; Winter-Spring 1973.

The Beach Boys in Concert goes gold as a double-record set; 1973-1974.

Endless Summer, a Capitol Records rerelease, goes number 1, drops off the charts, then climbs back on and hits number 20. After falling off again, it gains more popularity and spends 67 weeks on the charts, eventually going platinum; Summer 1974-Summer 1975.

Spirit of America, another Capitol "best of" reissue, spends 43 weeks on *Billboard's* charts, climbs to number 8; Summer 1975.

15 Big Ones cracks the top ten, with "Rock and Roll Music" climbing as high as number 5; Summer 1976.

The Beach Boys Love You gathers little attention, no promotion, and few sales; Spring 1977.

L.A. (Light Album), a disco-inspired LP released on Caribou Records, sells more than 400,000 copies, but alienates their traditional base of fans; March 1979.

Keepin' the Summer Alive spends six weeks on *Billboard's* charts, reaching number 76; Spring 1980.

The Beach Boys, on CBS Records, and *Golden Harmonies*, on Capitol Records—both compilations of old hits—are released to little critical or commercial acclaim; Summer 1985.

"Kokomo," released with the album *Still Cruisin'*, soars to number one in the U.S., becoming the first Beach Boys' top-rated hit in twenty-two years; June 1989.

DISCOGRAPHY

The most complete Beach Boys discography has been compiled by Brad Elliot in *Surf's Up: The Beach Boys on Record, 1961-1981* (Ann Arbor, MI.: Pierian Press, 1982.) Although now ten years out of date and requiring some revision, it still remains, in the author's own immodest but accurate assessment, "the ultimate reference book to the group's music, both released and unreleased" (p. 444). Elliott has clarified the confusing re-releases and anthologies and has also included various mail order only releases. *Surf's Up* is an extraordinarily helpful publication, but not always easy to find. The following is a list of albums released in the United States.

Surfin' Safari **(1962)**
[Capitol T 1808]

SIDE ONE

"Surfin' Safari" (B. Wilson—M. Love)
"County Fair" (B. Wilson—G. Usher)
"Ten Little Indians" (B. Wilson—G. Usher)
"Chug-A-Lug" (B. Wilson—G. Usher)
"Little Girl (You're My Miss America)" (V. Catalano—H. Alpert)
"409" (B. Wilson—G. Usher)

SIDE TWO

"Surfin'" (B. Wilson—M. Love)
"Heads You Win—Tails I Lose" (B. Wilson—G. Usher)
"Summertime Blues" (E. Cochran—J. Capehart)
"Cuckoo Clock" (B. Wilson—G. Usher)
"Moon Dawg" (D. Weaver)
"The Shift" (B. Wilson—M. Love)

Surfin' U.S.A. (1963)
[Capitol T 1890]

SIDE ONE

"Surfin' U.S.A." (C. Berry—B. Wilson, new lyrics)
"Farmer's Daughter" (B. Wilson)
"Miserlou" (N. Roubanis—F. Wise—M. Leeds—S.K. Russel)
"Stoked" (B. Wilson)
"Lonely Sea" (G. Usher—B. Wilson)
"Shut Down" (B. Wilson—R. Christian)

SIDE TWO

"Noble Surfer" (B. Wilson)
"Honky Tonk" (B. Doggett)
"Lana" (B. Wilson)
"Surf Jam" (C. Wilson)
"Let's Go Trippin'" (D. Dale)
"Finders Keepers" (B. Wilson)

Shut Down (1963)
[Capitol T 1918]

SIDE ONE

"Shut Down" (B. Wilson—R. Christian)
"Chicken" (J. Leiber—M. Stoller—J. Rollins)
"Wide Track" (G. Usher—R. Christian)
"Brontosaurus Stomp" (L. Mayorga—E. Cobb)
"Four On the Floor" (G. Usher—R. Christian)
"Black Denim Jacket and Motorcycle Boots"
    (J. Leiber—M. Stoller)

SIDE TWO

"409" (B. Wilson—G. Usher)
"Street Machine" (G. Usher—R. Christian)
"The Ballad of Thunder Road" (D. Raye—R. Mitchum)
"Hot Rod Race" (G. Wilson)
"Car Trouble" (E. McDuff—O. Couch)
"Cheater Slicks" (G. Usher—R. Christian)

This album contains only two songs performed by The Beach Boys, "Shut Down" and "409," both of which had been released earlier. To take advantage of the group's popularity, Capitol Records apparently rushed out this anthology of car songs, calling it a Beach Boys album.

Surfer Girl (1963)
[Capitol T 1981]

SIDE ONE

"Surfer Girl" (B. Wilson)
"Catch A Wave" (B. Wilson)
"The Surfer Moon" (B. Wilson)
"South Bay Surfer" (S. Foster—B. Wilson—D. Wilson—A. Jardine, new lyrics)
"The Rocking Surfer" (trad. arr. B. Wilson)
"Little Deuce Coupe" (B. Wilson—R. Christian)

SIDE TWO

"In My Room" (B. Wilson—G. Usher)
"Hawaii" (B. Wilson)
"Surfer's Rule" (B. Wilson—M. Love)
"Our Car Club" (B. Wilson—M. Love)
"Your Summer Dream" (B. Wilson—B. Norberg)
"Boogie Woogie" (Rimsky-Korsakov, arr. B. Wilson)

Little Deuce Coupe (1963)
[Capitol T 1998]

SIDE ONE

"Little Deuce Coupe" (B. Wilson—R. Christian)
"Ballad of Ole' Betsy" (B. Wilson—R. Christian)
"Be True To Your School" (B. Wilson)
"Car Crazy Cutie" (B. Wilson—R. Christian)
"Cherry, Cherry Coupe" (B. Wilson—R. Christian)
"409" (B. Wilson—R. Christian)

SIDE TWO

"Shut Down" (B. Wilson—R. Christian)
"Spirit of America" (B. Wilson—R. Christian)
"Our Car Club" (B. Wilson—M. Love)
"No-Go Showboat" (B. Wilson—R. Christian)
"A Young Man Is Gone" (B. Troup—M. Love, new lyrics)
"Custom Machine" (B. Wilson)

Shut Down, Volume 2 (1964)
[Capitol T 2027]
(re-issued as *Fun, Fun, Fun*
[Capitol SF 702])

SIDE ONE

"Fun, Fun, Fun" (B. Wilson—M. Love)
"Don't Worry Baby" (B. Wilson—R. Christian)
"In the Parking Lot" (B. Wilson—R. Christian)
" "Cassius" Love vs. "Sonny" Wilson" (M. Love—B. Wilson)
"The Warmth of the Sun" (B. Wilson—M. Love)
"This Car of Mine" (B. Wilson—M. Love)

SIDE TWO

"Why Do Fools Fall In Love?" (F. Lymon—G. Goldner)
"Pom-Pom Play Girl" (B. Wilson—M. Love)

"Keep An Eye On Summer" (B. Wilson—B. Norberg—Norman—M. Love)
"Shut Down, Part II" (C. Wilson)
"Louie, Louie" (R. Berry)
"Denny's Drums" (D. Wilson)

All Summer Long (1964)
[Capitol T 2110]

SIDE ONE

"I Get Around" (B. Wilson)
"All Summer Long" (B. Wilson)
"Hushabye" (D. Pomus—M. Schuman)
"Little Honda" (B. Wilson—M. Love)
"We'll Run Away" (B. Wilson—G. Usher)
"Carl's Big Chance" (B. Wilson—C. Wilson)

SIDE TWO

"Wendy" (B. Wilson)
"Do You Remember?" (B. Wilson)
"Girls On the Beach" (B. Wilson)
"Drive-In" (B. Wilson)
"Our Favorite Recording Sessions" (B. Wilson—D. Wilson—C. Wilson—M. Love—A. Jardine)
"Don't Back Down" (B. Wilson)

The Beach Boys Christmas Album (1964)
[Capitol T 2164]

SIDE ONE

"Little Saint Nick" (B. Wilson)
"The Man With All the Toys" (B. Wilson)
"Santa's Beard" (B. Wilson)
"Merry Christmas Baby" (B. Wilson)
"Christmas Day" (B. Wilson)

"Frosty the Snowman" (S. Nelson—J. Rollins)

SIDE TWO

"We Three Kings..." (John Henry Hopkins)
"Blue Christmas" (B. Hayes—J. W. Johnson)
"Santa Claus Is Comin' To Town" (J. F. Coots—H. Gillespie)
"White Christmas" (I. Berlin)
"I'll Be Home for Christmas" (K. Gannon—W. Kent—B. Ram)
"Auld Lang Syne" (trad.)

The Beach Boys in Concert (1964)
[Capitol TAO 2918]

SIDE ONE

"Fun, Fun, Fun" (B. Wilson—M. Love)
"The Little Old Lady From Pasadena"
    (D. Aetfield—R. Christian)
"Little Deuce Coupe" (B. Wilson—R. Christian)
"Long Tall Texan" (H. Strezlecki)
"In My Room" (B. Wilson—G. Usher)
"The Monster Mash" (L. Capizzi—B. Pickett)
"Let's Go Trippin'" (D. Dale)

SIDE TWO

"Papa-Oom-Mow-Mow" (A. Frazier—C. White—S. Harris—R. Wilson, Jr.)
"The Wanderer" (E. Maresca)
"Hawaii" (B. Wilson)
"Graduation Day" (J. Sherman—N. Sherman)
"I Get Around" (B. Wilson)
"Johnny B. Goode" (C. Berry)

The Beach Boys Today! (1965)
[Capitol T 2269]

SIDE ONE

"Do You Wanna Dance?" (B. Freeman)
"Good to My Baby" (B. Wilson)
"Don't Hurt My Little Sister" (B. Wilson)
"When I Grow Up" (B. Wilson)
"Help Me, Rhonda" (B. Wilson)
"Dance, Dance, Dance" (B. Wilson—C. Wilson)

SIDE TWO

"Please Let Me Wander" (B. Wilson—M. Love)
"I'm So Young" (W. H. Tyrus, Jr.)
"Kiss Me, Baby" (B. Wilson)
"She Knows Me Too Well" (B. Wilson)
"In the Back Of My Mind" (B. Wilson)
"Bull Session With Big Daddy" (B. Wilson—C. Wilson—D. Wilson—M. Love—A. Jardine)

Summer Days (and Summer Nights!!) (1965)
Capitol T 2354]

SIDE ONE

"The Girl From New York City" (B. Wilson)
"Amusement Parks U.S.A." (B. Wilson)
"Then I Kissed Her" (P. Spector—E. Greenwich—J. Barry)
"Salt Lake City" (B. Wilson)
"Girl, Don't Tell Me" (B. Wilson)
"Help Me, Rhonda" (B. Wilson)

SIDE TWO

"California Girls" (B. Wilson)
"Let Him Run Wild" (B. Wilson)

"You're So Good To Me" (B. Wilson)
"Summer Means New Love" (B. Wilson)
"I'm Bugged At My Old Man" (B. Wilson)
"And Your Dream Comes True" (M. Love—B. Wilson)

Beach Boys Party! (1965)
[Capitol MAS 2398]

SIDE ONE

"Hully Gully" (F. Smith—C. Goldsmith)
"I Should Have Known Better" (J. Lennon—P. McCartney)
"Tell Me Why" (J. Lennon—P. McCartney)
"Papa-Oom-Mow-Mow" (A. Frazier—C. White—S. Harris—R. Wilson, Jr.)
"Mountain Of Love" (H. Dorman)
"You've Got To Hide Your Love Away" (J. Lennon—P. McCartney)
"Devoted To You" (B. Bryant)

SIDE TWO

"Alley Oop" (D. Frazier)
"There's No Other (Like My Baby)" (P. Spector—L. Bates)
Medley: "I Get Around" (B. Wilson); "Little Deuce Coupe" (B. Wilson—R. Christian)
"The Times They Are A-Changin'" (B. Dylan)
"Barbara Ann" (F. Fassert)

Pet Sounds (1966)
[Capitol T 2458]

SIDE ONE

"Wouldn't It Be Nice" (B. Wilson—T. Asher)
"You Still Believe In Me" (B. Wilson—T. Asher)
"That's Not Me" (B. Wilson—T. Asher)
"Don't Talk (Put Your Head On My Shoulder)" (B. Wilson—T. Asher)

"I'm Waiting For the Day" (B. Wilson—M. Love)
"Let's Go Away For Awhile" (B. Wilson)
"Sloop John B." (arr. B. Wilson)

SIDE TWO

"God Only Knows" (B. Wilson—T. Asher)
"I Know There's An Answer" (B. Wilson—T. Sachen)
"Here Today" (B. Wilson—T. Asher)
"I Just Wasn't Made for These Times"
         (B. Wilson—T. Asher)
"Pet Sounds" (B. Wilson)
"Caroline, No" (B. Wilson—T. Asher)

Best of The Beach Boys [Volume 1] (1966)
[Capitol T 2545]

SIDE ONE

"Surfin' U.S.A."
"Catch A Wave"
"Surfer Girl"
"Little Deuce Coupe"
"In My Room"
"Little Honda"

SIDE TWO

"Fun, Fun, Fun"
"The Warmth of the Sun"
"Louie, Louie"
"Kiss Me, Baby"
"You're So Good To Me"
"Wendy"

Composers of the songs on this and the other *Best of The Beach Boys* anthologies are indicated under the albums on which the songs first appeared.

Best of The Beach Boys [Volume 2] (1967)
[Capitol T 2706]

SIDE ONE

"Barbara Ann"
"When I Grow Up"
"Long, Tall Texan"
"Please Let Me Wonder"
"Let Him Run Wild"

SIDE TWO

"Don't Worry Baby"
"Surfin' Safari"
"Little Saint Nick"
"California Girls"
"Help Me, Rhonda"
"I Get Around"

Smiley Smile (1967)
[Brother T 9001]

SIDE ONE

"Heroes and Villains" (B. Wilson—V. D. Parks)
"Vegetables" (B. Wilson—V. D. Parks)
"Fall Breaks and Back to Winter" (W. Woodpecker Symphony)
"She's Goin' Bald" (B. Wilson—M. Love—V. D. Parks)
"Little Pad" (B. Wilson)

SIDE TWO

"Good Vibrations" (B. Wilson—M. Love)
"With Me Tonight" (B. Wilson)
"Wind Chimes" (B. Wilson)
"Gettin' Hungry" (B. Wilson)
"Wonderful" (B. Wilson—V.D. Parks)
"Whistle In" (B. Wilson)

The Beach Boys Deluxe Set (1967)
[Capitol TCL 2813]

A three-album boxed set comprising *Pet Sounds, Summer Days (and Summer Nights!!)* and *Beach Boys Today!*. The entire set is issued in duophonic sound.

Wild Honey (1967)
[Capitol T 2859]

SIDE ONE

"Wild Honey" (B. Wilson—M. Love)
"Aren't You Glad?" (B. Wilson—M. Love)
"I Was Made to Love Her" (H. Cosby—Hardaway—S. Moy—S. Wonder)
"Country Air" (B. Wilson—M Love)
"A Thing or Two" (B. Wilson—M. Love)

SIDE TWO

"Darlin'" (B.Wilson—M. Love)
"I'd Love Just Once to See You" (B. Wilson—M. Love)
"Here Comes the Night" (B. Wilson—M. Love)
"Let the Wind Blow" (B. Wilson—M. Love)
"How She Boogalooed It" (M. Love—B. Johnston—A. Jardine—C. Wilson)
"Mama Says" (B. Wilson—M. Love)

Friends (1968)
[Capitol ST 2895]

SIDE ONE

"Meant For You" (B. Wilson—M. Love)
"Friends" (B. Wilson—D. Wilson—C. Wilson—A. Jardine)
"Wake the World" (B. Wilson—A. Jardine)

"Be Here In the Morning" (B. Wilson—D. Wilson—C. Wilson—M. Love—A. Jardine)
"When a Man Needs a Woman" (B. Wilson—D. Wilson—A. Jardine—S. Korthof—J. Parks)
"Passing By" (B. Wilson)

SIDE TWO

"Anna Lee, the Healer" (M. Love—B. Wilson)
"Little Bird" (D. Wilson—S. Kalinich)
"Be Still" (D. Wilson—S. Kalinich)
"Busy Doin' Nothin'" (B. Wilson)
"Diamond Head" (A. Vescozo—L. Ritz—J. Ackley—B. Wilson)
"Transcendental Meditation" (B. Wilson—M. Love—A. Jardine)

Stack O' Tracks (1968)
[Capitol DKAO 2893]

SIDE ONE

"Darlin'"
"Salt Lake City"
"Sloop John B."
"In My Room"
"Catch A Wave"
"Wild Honey"
"Little Saint Nick"

SIDE TWO

"Do It Again"
"Wouldn't It Be Nice"
"God Only Knows"
"Surfer Girl"
"Little Honda"
"Here Today"
"You're So Good to Me"
"Let Him Run Wild"
"Their Original Backing Tracks to the Songs"

The Best of The Beach Boys [Volume 3] (1969)
[Capitol SKAO 2945]

SIDE ONE

"God Only Knows"
"Dance, Dance, Dance"
"409"
"The Little Girl I Once Knew"
"Frosty the Snowman"
"Girl, Don't Tell Me"

SIDE TWO

"Surfin'"
"Heroes and Villains"
"She Knows Me Too Well"
"Darlin'"
"Good Vibrations"

20/20 (1969)
[Capitol SKAO 133]

SIDE ONE

"Do It Again" (B. Wilson—M. Love)
"I Can Hear Music" (J. Barry—P. Spector—E. Greenwich)
"Bluebirds Over the Mountain" (E. Hickey)
"Be With Me" (D. Wilson)
"All I Want to Do" (D. Wilson)
"The Nearest Faraway Place" (B. Johnston)

SIDE TWO

"Cotton Fields" (H. Ledbetter)
"I Went to Sleep" (B. Wilson—C. Wilson)
"Time to Get Alone" (B. Wilson)
"Never Learn Not to Love" (D. Wilson)
"Our Prayer" (B. Wilson)
"Cabinessence" (B. Wilson—V. D. Parks)

Sunflower (1970)
[Brother RS 6382]

SIDE ONE

"Slip On Through" (D. Wilson)
"This Whole World" (B. Wilson)
"Add Some Music to Your Day" (B. Wilson—J. Knott—M. Love)
"Got to Know the Woman" (D. Wilson)
"Deirdre" (B. Johnston—B. Wilson)
"It's About Time" (D. Wilson—B. Burchman—A. Jardine)

SIDE TWO

"Tears In the Morning" (B. Johnston)
"All I Wanna Do" (B. Wilson—M. Love)
"Forever" (D. Wilson—G. Jacobson)
"Our Sweet Love" (B. Wilson—C. Wilson—A. Jardine)
"At My Window" (A. Jardine—B. Wilson)
"Cool, Cool Water" (B. Wilson—M. Love)

Surf's Up (1971)
[Brother/Reprise RS 6453]

SIDE ONE

"Don't Go Near the Water" (A. Jardine—M. Love)
"Long Promised Road" (C. Wilson—J. Rieley)
"Take a Load Off Your Feet" (A. Jardine—G. Winfrey—B. Wilson)
"Disney Girls (1957)" (B. Johnston)
"Student Demonstration Time" (Based on "Riot In Cell Block No. 9" by J. Leiber and M. Stoller; new lyrics by M. Love)

SIDE TWO

"Feel Flows" (C. Wilson—J. Rieley)
"Lookin' At Tomorrow (A Welfare Song)" (A. Jardine—G. Winfrey)
"A Day In the Life Of a Tree" (B. Wilson—J. Rieley)
"Till I Die" (B. Wilson)

"Surf's Up" (B. Wilson—V. D. Parks)

Carl and The Passions—So Tough (1972)
[Brother/Reprise 2MS 2083]

SIDE ONE

"You Need a Mess of Help to Stand Alone" (B. Wilson—J. Rieley)
"Here She Comes" (R. Fataar—B. Chapin)
"He Come Down" (A. Jardine—B. Wilson—M. Love)
"Marcella" (B.Wilson—J. Rieley)

SIDE TWO

"Hold On, Dear Brother" (R. Fataar—B. Chapin)
"Make It Good" (D. Wilson—D. Dragon)
"All This Is That" (A. Jardine—C. Wilson—M.Love)
"Cuddle Up" (D. Wilson—D. Dragon)

This album was released with *Pet Sounds*, but this time, according to the album, *Pet Sounds* is heard in monophonic sound, the way it was originally produced.

Holland (1973)
[Brother/Reprise MS 2118]

SIDE ONE

"Sail On, Sailor" (B. Wilson—T. Almar; lyricists: J. Rieley—R. Kennedy)
"Steamboat" (D. Wilson—J. Rieley)
"California Saga"
    Part One: "Big Sur" (M. Love)
    Part Two: "The Beaks Of the Eagles" (R. Jeffers, from "Jeffers County;" composers and additional lyrics: A. Jardine—L. Jardine)
    Part Three: "California" (A. Jardine)

SIDE TWO

"The Trader" (C. Wilson—J. Rieley)
"Leavin' This Town" (R. Fataar—C. Wilson—B. Chapin—M. Love)
"Only With You" (D. Wilson—M. Love)
"Funky Pretty" (B. Wilson—M. Love; add. lyrics J. Rieley)

"Mount Vernon and Fairway"—A Fairy Tale in Several Parts (B. Wilson; add. material J. Rieley) comprises a seven-inch LP included with the album.

The Beach Boys in Concert (1973)
[Brother 2RS 6484]

SIDE ONE

"Sail On, Sailor"
"Sloop John B."
"The Trader"
"You Still Believe In Me"
"California Girls"
"Darlin'"

SIDE TWO

"Marcella"
"Caroline, No"
"Leavin' This Town"
"Heroes And Villains"

SIDE THREE

"Funky Pretty"
"Let the Wind Blow"
"Help Me, Rhonda"
"Surfer Girl"
"Wouldn't It Be Nice"

SIDE FOUR

"We Got Love"
"Don't Worry Baby"
"Surfin' U.S.A."
"Good Vibrations"
"Fun, Fun, Fun"

15 Big Ones (1976)
[Brother/Reprise MS 2251]

SIDE ONE

"Rock and Roll Music" (C. Berry)
"It's O.K." (B. Wilson—M. Love)
"Had to Phone Ya'" (B. Wilson—M. Love) [D. Rovell is credited on the LP, but Elliot omits her in his listing]
"Chapel of Love" (J. Barry—E. Greenwich—P. Spector)
"Everyone's In Love With You" (M. Love)
"Talk to Me" (J. Seneca)/"Tallahassie Lassie" (F. Slay, Jr.—B. Crewe—F. Piscariello)
"That Same Song" (B. Wilson—M. Love)
"TM Song" (B. Wilson)

SIDE TWO

"Palisades Park" (C. Barris)
"Susie Cincinnati" (A. Jardine)
"A Casual Look" (E. Wells)
"Blueberry Hill" (A. Lewis—L. Stock—V. Rose)
"Back Home" (B. Wilson)
"In the Still Of the Night" (F. Parris)
"Just Once In My Life" (G. Goffin—C. King—P. Spector)

The Beach Boys Love You (1977)
[Brother/Reprise MSK 2258]

SIDE ONE

"Let Us Go On This Way" (B. Wilson—M. Love)
"Roller Skating Child" (B. Wilson)
"Mona" (B. Wilson)
"Johnny Carson" (B. Wilson)
"Good Time" (B. Wilson—A. Jardine)
"Honkin' Down the Highway" (B. Wilson)

SIDE TWO

"Ding Dong" (B. Wilson-R. McGuinn)
"Solar System" (B. Wilson)
"The Night Was So Young" (B. Wilson)
"I'll Bet He's Nice" (B. Wilson)
"Let's Put Our Hearts Together" (B. Wilson)
"I Wanna Pick You Up" (B. Wilson)
"Airplane" (B. Wilson)
"Love Is A Woman" (B. Wilson)

MIU Album (1978)
[Brother/Reprise MSK 2268]

SIDE ONE

"She's Got Rhythm" (B. Wilson—M. Love—R. Altbach)
"Come Go With Me" (C.E. Quick)
"Hey, Little Tomboy" (B. Wilson)
"Kona Coast" (A. Jardine—M. Love)
"Peggy Sue" (J. Allison—N. Petty—B. Holly)
"Wontcha Come Out Tonight" (B. Wilson—M. Love)

SIDE TWO

"Sweet Sunday Kind Of Love" (B. Wilson—M. Love)
"Belles of Paris" (B. Wilson—M. Love—R. Altbach)

"Pitter Patter" (B. Wilson—M. Love—R. Altbach)
"My Diane" (B. Wilson)
"Match Point of Our Love" (B. Wilson—M. Love)
"Winds of Change" (R. Altbach—E. Tuleja)

L.A. (Light Album) (1979)
[Caribou JZ 35752]

SIDE ONE

"Good Timin'" (B. Wilson—C. Wilson)
"Lady Lynda" (A. Jardine—R. Altbach)
"Full Sail" (C. Wilson—G. Cushing-Murray)
"Angel, Come Home" (C. Wilson—G. Cushing-Murray)
"Love Surrounds Me" (D. Wilson—G. Cushing-Murray)
"Sumahama" (M. Love)

SIDE TWO

"Here Comes the Night" (B. Johnston—C. Becher)
"Baby Blue" (D. Wilson—G. Jacobson—K. Lamm)
"Goin' South" (C. Wilson—G. Cushing-Murray)
"Shortenin' Bread" (arr. B. Wilson)

Keepin' the Summer Alive (1980)
[Caribou JZ 36283]

SIDE ONE

"Keepin' the Summer Alive" (C. Wilson—R. Bachman)
"Oh Darlin'" (B. Wilson—M. Love)
"Some of Your Love" (B. Wilson—M. Love)
"Livin' With a Heartache" (C. Wilson—R. Bachman)
"School Day" (C. Berry)

SIDE TWO

"Goin' On" (B. Wilson—M. Love)

"Sunshine" (B. Wilson—M. Love)
"When Girls Get Together" (B. Wilson—M. Love)
"Santa Ana Winds" (B. Wilson—A. Jardine)
"Endless Harmony" (B. Johnston)

Beach Boys/Brian Wilson Rarities (1981)
[Capitol ST-26463]

SIDE ONE

"Be True to Your School"
"Pamela Jean" (B. Wilson)
"Sacramento" (B. Wilson—B. Usher)
"The One You Can't Have" (B. Wilson)
"Thinkin' 'Bout You, Baby" (B. Wilson—M. Love)
"Guess I'm Dumb" (B. Wilson—T. Titelman)
"After the Game" (B. Wilson)
"Pray for Surf" (S. Glantz—D. Rovell)
"Runaround Lover" (B. Wilson—M. Love)
"Surfin' Down the Sewanee River" (S. Foster; new lyrics by B. Wilson)

SIDE TWO

"Cotton Fields" (H. Ledbetter, arr. A. Jardine)
"Lady" (D. Wilson)
"Celebrate the News" (D. Wilson—G. Jakobson)
"Sound Of Free" (D. Wilson—M. Love)
"Bluebirds Over the Mountain" (E. Hickey)
"Well, You're Welcome" (B. Wilson)
"The Lord's Prayer" (A. Malotte)
"The Story of My Life" (B. Wilson—M. Love)
"Goodnight My Love" (Motola-Mareskola)
"What I'd Say" (R. Charles)

The Beach Boys (1983)
[Capitol Records]

SIDE ONE

"Sloop John B."
"Catch A Wave"
"The Warmth of the Sun"
"Wild Honey"

SIDE TWO

"409"
"Hushabye"
"Don't Back Down"
"Why Do Fools Fall in Love?"
"Summer Means New Love"

Beach Boys (1985)
[Caribou BFZ 39946]

SIDE ONE

"Getcha Back" (M. Love—T. Melcher)
"It's Getting Late" (C. Wilson—M. Schilling—R. Johnson)
"Crack At Your Love" (B. Wilson—A. Jardine—E. Landy)
"Maybe I Don't Know" (C. Wilson—M. Schilling—S. Levine—J. Lindsay)
"She Believes In Love Again" (B. Johnston)

SIDE TWO

"California Calling" (A. Jardine—B. Wilson)
"Passing Friends" (G. O'Dowd—R. Hay)
"I'm So Lonely" (B. Wilson—E. Landy)
"Where I Belong" (C. Wilson—R. Johnson)
"I Do Love You" (S. Wonder)
"It's Just a Matter of Time" (B. Wilson—E. Landy)

Golden Harmonies (1985)
[Capitol Records PDK2 1084]

SIDE ONE

"Help Me, Rhonda"
"Dance, Dance, Dance"
"When I Grow Up (To Be A Man)"
"Johnny B. Goode"
"Fun, Fun, Fun,"
"Keep An Eye On Summer"
"409"
"Pet Sounds"

SIDE TWO

"Little Deuce Coupe"
"Do You Wanna Dance?"
"Sloop John B."
"Shut Down"
"Surfin' U.S.A."
"The Little Old Lady From Pasadena"
"The Wanderer"
"Surfin'"

California (and Other) Girls (1987)
[Capitol Records]

SIDE ONE

"Darlin'"
"Barbara Ann"
"Wendy"
"Girl, Don't Tell Me"
"The Girl From New York City"

SIDE TWO

"California Girls"

"Surfer Girl"
"Little Girl I Once Knew"
"Girls On the Beach"

Still Cruisin' (1989)
[Capitol Records C4 92639]

SIDE ONE

"Still Cruisin'" (T. Melcher—M. Love)
"Somewhere Near Japan" (J. Phillips—T. Melcher—M. Love—B. Johnston)
"Island Girl" (A. Jardine)
"In My Car" (B. Wilson—E. Landy—A. Morgan)
"Kokomo" (J. Phillips—M. Love—T. Melcher—S. McKenzie)

SIDE TWO

"Wipe Out" (The Surfaris)
"Make It Big" (T. Melcher—B. House—M. Love)
"I Get Around"
"Wouldn't It Be Nice"
"California Girls"

This album is mostly a compilation of new songs recorded for six different films. The remake of "Wipe Out" was recorded with the rap group The Fat Boys.

In addition to the recordings listed here, there are several anthology albums available on separate labels. Only one, however, merits the interest of anyone collecting Beach Boys music—the album including their earliest work:

The Best of The Beach Boys

SIDE ONE

"Surfer Girl"
"Barbee" (Morgan)
"Luau" (Morgan)
"Little Deuce Coupe"
"Surfin'"

SIDE TWO

"Surfin' Safari"
"Judy" (B. Wilson)
"What Is a Young Girl?" (Morgan)
"409"
"Karate" (B. Wilson)

This album has appeared on at least three different labels: Scepter, Springboard, and Orbit. The contents remain the same.

Other anthologies issued both in the United States and abroad exist, but the material in every case simply repeats what is available elsewhere. One import album does bear mention, however—a concert recorded at the London Palladium:

Live in London (1970)
[Capitol ST 21715]

SIDE ONE

"Darlin'"
"Wouldn't It Be Nice"
"Sloop John B."
"California Girls"
"Do It Again"
"Wake the World"
"Aren't You Glad?"

SIDE TWO

"Bluebirds Over the Mountains"
"Their Hearts Were Full Of Spring"
"Good Vibrations"
"God Only Knows"
"Barbara Ann"

BIBLIOGRAPHY

The older tendency among rock 'n' roll historians, like Greil Marcus in *Mystery Train: Images of America in Rock 'n' Roll Music* (originally published in 1975), to patronize The Beach Boys has been eroding over the past fifteen years. A number of full-length studies now exist, and the old prejudice against their "cool" and polish—as opposed to those performers who suggest if not reveal, emotional depth and raw power in their writing and/or performing—is now diminishing.

Barnes, Ken. *The Beach Boys*, ed. Greg Shaw. New York: Sire Books, Chappell Music Company, 1976. An early study that might be responsible for the emphasis on photographs featured in nearly every subsequent book on the group.

Belz, Carl. *The Story of Rock*. New York: Oxford University Press, 1969, p. 96-101. The Beach Boys are treated as an extension of folk music. Even though the group recorded several albums after the date of his first edition, Belz takes no note of this work in his second edition, issued in 1972.

Christgau, Robert. *Any Old Way You Choose It: Rock and Other Pop Music, 1966-73*. Baltimore: Penguin Books, Inc., 1973. Scattered throughout this collection of essays and reviews are incisive remarks on The Beach Boys. Unfortunately, no single article focuses on them specifically.

Cohn, Nik. *Rock: From the Beginning*. New York: Stein and Day, 1969, p. 118-123. This is an overstated, hyper-description of the group's surfing and car music from an English writer's point of view. Entertaining to read, but not always accurate.

Edmonds, Ben. "The Beach Boys," in *Rock Revolution*, edited by Richard Robinson *et al.* New York: Curtis Books, 1973, p. 75-77. Favorable criticism of their work, mostly about *Pet Sounds*.

Elliot, Brad. *Surf's Up: The Beach Boys on Record, 1961-1981*. Ann Arbor, Mich.: Pierian Press, 1982. The most authoritative and complete listing of Beach Boys' records.

Gabree, John. *The World of Rock*. Greenwich, Conn.: Fawcett Books, 1968, p. 143-144. The first book-length essay on rock music; not as informative as Arnold Shaw's study—which appeared the following year—but more opinionated. The Beach Boys are complimented, but the criticism is reductive.

Gaines, Steven. *Heroes and Villains: The True Story of the Beach Boys*. London: Macmillan London Ltd., 1986. Written in a gratuitous, behind the scenes, you-were-there narrative style that details the drugs, sex, booze and fisticuffs the group went through. The Beach Boys are praised, but in such an idolatrous tone that it reads more like a book-length fan magazine than a "true story," and there is precious little discussion of their music.

Gillett, Charlie. *The Sound of the City: The Rise of Rock and Roll*, Rev. ed. New York: Dell Books, 1972, p. 293-294. This is the fullest study of the subject, but it describes The Beach Boys only as a "surfing sound" group, ignoring their development beyond 1965.

Jahn, Mike. *Rock: From Elvis Presley to the Rolling Stones*. New York: Quadrangle/The New York Times Book Co., 1973. Because the book is arranged chronologically, his discussion of The Beach Boys is disjointed, repetitious, and not always accurate. Written in a cloying style, Jahn's argument stresses the superficial quality of the lyrics while underestimating their musical achievement.

Landau, Jon. *It's Too Late to Stop Now: A Rock and Roll Journal*. San Francisco: Straight Arrow Books, 1972, p. 82-86. A valuable description of their 1971 Boston Symphony Hall concert, along with a positive appraisal of their work up to that time. A short, but favorable, review of *Surf's Up* follows.

Leaf, David. *The Beach Boys and the California Myth*. New York: Grosset & Dunlap, 1978. An interesting chronological look at The Beach Boys and how the band became so popular and unique. Some useful insights into the creation of their music, particularly into Brian Wilson.

Milward, John. *The Beach Boys: Silver Anniversary*. Garden City, NY: Doubleday/Dolphin, 1985. An excellent, balanced study beautifully produced with the best and most interesting photographs. With a brief but helpful discography and bibliography as well.

Nolan, Tom. "The Beach Boys: A California Saga," in *Rolling Stone* no. 94 (Oct. 28, 1971): 32-39; and no. 95 (Nov. 11, 1971): 50-52, with additional material by David Felton. The first part is valuable for the remarks of Nick Venet, who signed the group for Capitol. He points out Brian Wilson's importance in opening up the California recording industry, and helping to make it a center for innovation. The second part is mostly an interview with Murray Wilson, the father of the three Beach Boys. If the members of the group have become reclusive, these articles suggest why.

Preiss, Byron. *The Beach Boys*. New York: St. Martin's Press, 1983 (originally published in 1978). More interesting for its illustrations, especially in the 1978 edition, than for its text. Produced with the authorization and cooperation of The Beach Boys.

Roxon, Lillian. *Rock Encyclopedia*. New York: Grosset & Dunlap, 1971. A fundamental book. Although it slights some important figures from the late fifties and early sixties, Roxon treats The Beach Boys seriously, with both accuracy and respect. She lists a helpful but not entirely accurate discography through 1969.

Shannon, Bob and John Javna. *Behind the Hits*. New York: Warner Books, Ltd., 1986, p. 144, 193. (Not seen.)

Shaw, Arnold. *The Rock Revolution*. New York: Paperback Library, 1971 (originally published 1969), p. 156-159. An accurate, perceptive and generally informative book, not only on The Beach Boys, but on popular music in general.

Stars and Superstars of Rock. London: Octopus Book Ltd., 1974, p. 144-148. Recently, several oversized picture books from England on rock music have been made available in this country. This compilation is opinionated, but interesting; unfortunately, certain errors betray careless writing (Hawthorne, California is near Los Angeles, not San Francisco, for example). It is valuable for its illustrations, however.

Tobler, John. *The Beach Boys.* London: Phoebus Publishing Co., 1978. An insightful if somewhat glossy look at the band. Particulary interesting for its anecdotes about how and why some of the songs were composed, and especially their reception in England. A chatty, quick-read of a book that has some useful musical analysis.

Williams, Paul. *Outlaw Blues: A Book of Rock Music.* New York: E. P. Dutton & Co., 1969, p. 117-169. A long conversation with Dave Anderle, this piece rambles in celebrating Brian Wilson's talent. One of the most adulatory writings on The Beach Boys ever published.

NOTES

1. Shaw, Arnold, *The Rockin' 50's* (New York: Hawthorn Books, Inc., 1974), p. 137. An interview with Haley follows.

2. Hopkins, Jerry, *Elvis: A Biography* 1971 (New York: Warner Paperback Library, 1972), p. 127-128.

3. Stearns, Marshall and Jean, *Jazz Dance: The Story of American Vernacular Dance* (New York: The MacMillen Company, London: Collier-MacMillan, Ltd., 1968).

4. Poggioli, Renato, *The Oaten Flute: Essays on Pastoral Poetry and the Pastoral Ideal* (Cambridge, Mass.: Harvard University Press, 1975).

5. Marx, Leo, *The Machine in the Garden: Technology and the Pastoral Ideal in America* (New York: Oxford University Press, 1964).

6. Nolan, Tom, "The Beach Boys: A California Saga," *Rolling Stone*, No. 94 (Oct. 28, 1971): p. 32-39. The record producer in this case is Terry Melcher.

7. Marcus, Greil, *Mystery Train: Images of America in Rock 'n' Roll Music* (New York: E. P. Dutton and Co., Inc., 1975), p. 26. The tradition goes as far back as Robert Johnson's "Terraplane Blues."

8. *The Beach Boys Christmas Album* used a full orchestra, but Brian Wilson did none of the arrangements.

9. *Op. cit.*, Nolan.

10. Bugliosi, Vincent, with Curt Gentry, *Helter Skelter: The True Story of the Manson Murders* (New York: W. W. Norton and Co., Inc., 1974), p. 250-251.

11. *Op. cit.*, Poggioli. The author argues that, psychologically, the pastoral represents a two-fold yearning after both happiness and innocence, states of mind attainable by retreating without undergoing either conversion or regeneration.

12. Fitzgerald, F. Scott, *The Great Gatsby*. See the conclusion for a striking use of reference to Holland as a perspective from which to gaze upon America. "And as the moon rose higher the inessential houses began to melt away until gradually I became aware of the old island here that had flowered once for Dutch sailor's eyes—a fresh, green breast of the new world." Greil Marcus partially quotes this passage in his work cited above, contending that much of rock 'n' roll music emphasizes "The promise of American life" (p. 22).

13. Grotke, J. Dean, "The Beach Boys earn a big response," *San Bernardino Sun*, 17 Sept. 1990, p. D6.

INDEX

SONG AND ALBUM TITLES

Abbey Road, 41
"Add Some Music to Your Day," 39, 68
"After the Game," 74
"Airplane," 72
"All I Wanna Do," 68
All Summer Long, 24-25, 28, 51, 59
"All Summer Long," 59
"All This Is That," 69
"Amusement Parks, U.S.A.," 61
"And Your Dream Comes True," 62
"Angel, Come Home," 73
"Aren't You Glad?" 65, 78
"At My Window," 68
"Baby Blue," 73
"Back Home," 71
"Barbara Ann," 52, 62, 64, 76, 79
"Be Here In the Morning," 38, 66
"Be True to Your School," 51, 58, 74
Beach Boys, 6, 43, 51, 53, 75
Beach Boys/Brian Wilson Rarities, 74
Beach Boys Christmas Album, 59, 84
The Beach Boys Deluxe Set, 65
The Beach Boys in Concert, 25, 53, 60, 70
The Beach Boys Love You, 43, 53, 72
Beach Boys Party!, 27, 30, 32, 52, 62
The Beach Boys Today!, 27-29, 61
"Belles of Paris," 72
Best of The Beach Boys, 52, 78
Best of The Beach Boys [Volume 1], 52, 63
Best of The Beach Boys [Volume 2], 52, 64

87

Best of the Beach Boys [Volume 3], 67
"Black Denim Jacket and Motorcycle Boots," 56
"Blueberry Hill," 71
"Bluebirds Over the Mountains," 6 52, 67, 74, 79
"Boogie Woogie," 57
"Brontosaurus Stomp," 56
"Busy Doin' Nothin'," 38-39, 66
California (and Other) Girls, 76
"California Calling," 75
"California Girls," 30, 45, 52, 61, 64, 70, 76, 77, 78
"California Saga," 42, 69
Carl and the Passions—So Tough, 53, 69
"Carl's Big Chance," 59
"Caroline, No," 35, 52, 63, 70
"A Casual Look," 71
" "Cassius" Love Vs. "Sonny" Wilson," 58
"Catch A Wave," 24-25, 43, 57, 63, 66, 75
"Celebrate the News," 74
"Chapel of Love," 71
"Christmas Day," 59
"Come Go With Me," 72
"Cool, Cool Water," 40, 68
"Cotton Fields," 39, 67, 74
"Country Air," 38, 40, 65 [or Fair]
"Crack At Your Love," 75
"Crazy, Man, Crazy," 13
"Cuddle Up," 69
"Dance, Dance, Dance," 29, 51, 61, 67, 76
"Darlin'," 65-67, 70, 76, 78
"Deirdre," 68
"Ding Dong," 72
"Do It Again," 38, 66, 67, 78
"Do You Wanna Dance?" 52, 61, 76
"Don't Back Down," 25, 59, 75
"Don't Go Near the Water," 40, 68
"Don't Hurt My Little Sister," 28, 61
"Don't Worry Baby," 58, 64, 71
"Drive-In," 59
"Endless Harmony," 74
"Everyone's In Love With You," 71

"Fall Breaks and Back to Winter," 37, 64
"Feel Flows," 40, 68
Fifteen (15) Big Ones, 43, 53, 71
"Forever," 68
Four "409," 22-24, 43, 55, 56, 57, 58, 67, 75, 76, 78
"Four On the Floor," 56
Friends, 38, 65
"Friends," 65
"Frosty the Snowman," 60, 67
"Full Sail," 73
Fun, Fun, Fun, 58
"Fun, Fun, Fun," 10, 23, 25, 29, 51, 58, 60, 63, 71, 76
"Funky Pretty," 71
"Getcha Back," 75
"Gettin' Hungry," 37, 64
"Girl, Don't Tell Me," 61, 67, 76
"The Girl From New York City," 30, 61, 76
"Girls On the Beach," 25, 59, 77
"God Only Knows," 34, 63, 66, 67, 79
"Goin' On," 73
"Goin' South," 73
Golden Harmonies, 43, 53, 76
"Good Time," 72
"Good Timin'" 73
"Goodnight My Love," 74
"Good to My Baby," 28, 61
"Good Vibrations," 6, 35-37, 47, 52, 64, 67, 71, 79
"Got to Know the Woman," 68
"Graduation Day, 25, 60
"Great Balls of Fire," 15
"Guess I'm Dumb," 74
"Had To Phone Ya," 71
"Hawaii," 57, 60
"He Come Down," 69
"Help Me, Rhonda," 6, 10, 29, 44, 47, 52, 61, 64, 70, 76
"Help!," 29
"Here Comes the Night," 43, 65, 73
"Here She Comes," 69
"Here Today," 34, 63, 66
"Heroes and Villains," 36-37, 52, 64, 67, 70

"Hey, Little Tomboy," 72
"Hold On, Dear Brother," 69
Holland, 12, 42, 45, 53, 69
"Honkin' Down the Highway," 72
"How She Boogalooed It," 65
"Hushabye," 59, 75
"I Can Hear Music," 67
"I Do Love You," 75
"I Get Around," 6, 10, 24, 45, 52, 59, 60, 62, 64, 77
"I Just Wasn't Made for These Times," 35, 63
"I Know There's An Answer," 63
"I Wanna Pick You Up," 72
"I Went to Sleep," 39, 67
"I'd Love Just Once to See You," 30, 65
"I'll Bet He's Nice," 72
"I'm Bugged At My Old Man," 30, 62
"I'm So Lonely," 75
"I'm Waiting for the Day," 34, 63
"In My Room," 25, 57, 60, 63, 66
"In the Parking Lot," 58
"In the Still of the Night," 71
"It's About Time," 68
"It's Getting Late," 75
"It's Just a Matter of Time," 75
"It's O.K.," 71
"Johnny B. Goode," 25, 60, 76
"Johnny Carson," 72
"Judy," 20, 78
"Just Once in My Life," 71
"Karate," 78
"Keep An Eye On Summer," 59, 76
Keepin' the Summer Alive, 53, 73
"Keepin' the Summer Alive," 73
"Kiss Me, Baby," 61, 63
"Kokomo," 8, 43-45, 54, 77
"Kona Coast," 72
L.A. (Light Album), 43, 53, 73
"Lady," 74
"Lady Linda," 73
"Leavin' This Town," 70

"Let Him Run Wild," 61, 64, 66
"Let the Wind Blow," 65, 70
"Let Us Go On this Way," 72
"Let's Go Away For Awhile," 63
"Let's Put Our Hearts Together," 72
Little Deuce Coupe, 6, 23-24, 58
"Little Deuce Coupe," 24, 51, 57, 58, 60, 62, 63, 76, 78
"The Little Girl I Once Knew," 67, 77
"Little Honda," 59, 63, 66
"The Little Old Lady From Pasadena," 60, 76
"Little Pad," 64
"Little Saint Nick," 59, 64, 66
Live in London, 78-79
"Livin' With a Heartache," 73
"Long Promised Road," 40, 68
"The Lord's Prayer," 74
"Louie, Louie," 59, 63
"Love Is A Woman," 72
"Love Surrounds Me," 73
"Make It Big," 46, 77
"Make It Good," 69
"Mama Says," 65
"The Man With All the Toys," 59
"Marcella," 69, 70
"Match Point of Our Love," 73
"Maybe I Don't Know," 75
"Meant For You," 65
"Merry Christmas Baby," 59
MIU Album, 43, 72
"Mona," 72
"Moon Dawg," 20-21, 55
"My Diane," 73
"The Night Was So Young," 72
"No Money Down," 15
"Noble Surfer," 56
"No-Go Showboat," 58
"Oh Darlin'," 73
"The One You Can't Have," 74
"Our Car Club," 57, 58
"Our Favorite Recording Sessions," 59

"Our Sweet Love," 39, 68
"Palisades Park," 71
"Pamela Jean," 75
"Passing Friends," 75
"Peggy Sue," 72
Pet Sounds, 31-35, 40, 49, 52-53, 62, 65, 69, 81
"Pet Sounds," 63, 76
"Pitter Patter, 73
"Pom-Pom Play Girl," 58
"Pray for Surf," 74
"Rock and Roll Music," 53, 71
"Rock Around the Clock," 13
"The Rocking Surfer," 57
"Roller Skating Child," 72
"Runaround Lover," 74
"Sacramento," 74
"Sail On, Sailor," 42, 69, 70
"Salt Lake City," 30, 61, 66
"Santa Ana Winds," 74
"Santa's Beard," 59
"School Day," 15, 29, 73
"See You Later, Alligator, 13
"She Believes In Love Again," 75
"She Knows Me Too Well," 61, 67
"She's Goin' Bald," 30, 37, 64
"She's Got Rhythm," 72
"The Shift," 21, 55
"Shortenin' Bread" 73
Shut Down, 22, 56
Shut Down, Volume 2, 24, 58
"Shut Down," 24, 51, 56, 57, 58, 76
"Shut Down, Part II," 59
"Skinny Minny," 13
"Sloop John B.," 34, 43, 52, 63, 66, 70, 75, 76, 78
Smiley Smile, 6, 37, 39, 52, 64
"Solar System," 72
"Some of Your Love," 73
"Sound of Free," 74
"South Bay Surfer," 57
Spirit of America, 43, 53,

"Spirit of America," 58
Stack O' Tracks, 66
"Steamboat, 42, 69
Still Cruisin', 43-46, 54, 77
"Still Cruisin'," 44, 77
"The Story of My Life," 74
"Susie Cincinnati," 71
"Sumahama," 73
Summer Days (and Summer Nights!!), 27, 30, 61, 65
Summer Means Fun, 19-20
"Summer Means New Love," 30, 62, 75
"Sunshine," 74
"Surf Jam," 56
Surfer Girl, 24, 51, 57
"Surfer Girl," 51, 57, 63, 66, 70, 77, 78
"The Surfer Moon," 57
"Surfer Stomp," 20
"Surfer's Rule," 57
"Surfin'," 5, 17, 20, 44, 51, 55, 67, 76, 78
"Surfin' Down the Sewanee River," 74
Surfin' Safari, 20-21, 55
"Surfin' Safari," 5, 17, 20, 47, 51, 55, 64, 78
Surfin' U.S.A., 5, 51, 56
"Surfin' U.S.A.," 19, 21-22, 24, 51, 56, 63, 71, 76
Surf's Up, 40-42, 53, 68, 81
"Surf's Up," 41, 69
"Sweet Sunday Kind of Love," 72
"Talk to Me," 71
"Tears In the Morning," 68
"Ten Little Indians," 55
"That Same Song," 71
"Their Hearts Were Full of Spring," 79
"Then I Kissed Her," 61
"There's No Other (Like My Baby)," 62
"Thinkin' 'Bout You, Baby," 74
"This Car of Mine," 58
"Till I Die, 41, 68
"Time to Get Alone," 67
"TM Song," 71
"The Trader," 70

"Transcendental Meditation," 38, 66
Twenty (20/20), 38-39, 52, 67
"Vegetables," 30, 37, 64
"Wake the World," 65, 78
"The Wanderer," 60, 76
"The Warmth of the Sun," 58, 63, 75
"We Got Love," 71
"We Three Kings...," 60
"Well, You're Welcome," 74
"Wendy," 28, 59, 63, 76
"What I'd Say," 74
"What Is a Young Girl?" 78
"When Girls Get Together," 74
"When I Grow Up (To Be A Man)," 29, 51, 61, 64, 76
"Whistle In," 64
"Whole Lot of Shakin' Goin' On," 15
"Why Do Fools Fall in Love?" 43, 58, 75
"Wide Track," 56
Wild Honey, 37, 43, 52, 65
"Wild Honey," 43, 65, 66, 75
"Wind Chimes," 37, 64
"Winds of Change," 73
"Wipe Out," 45, 77
"With Me Tonight," 64
"Wonderful," 64
"Wontcha Come Out Tonight," 72
"Wouldn't It Be Nice," 33-34, 45, 62, 66, 70, 77, 78
"Yakety Yak," 15
"You Need a Mess Of Help to Stand Alone," 69
"You Still Believe in Me," 33, 62, 70
"A Young Man Is Gone," 58
"Your Summer Dream," 57
"You're So Good to Me," 28, 62, 63, 66

INDIVIDUALS, GROUPS, AND SUBJECTS

ABC-TV, 7
Ackley, J., 66
Aetfield, D., 60

Almar, T., 69
Alpert, H., 55
Altbach, R., 73
American Graffiti [film], 24
Amsterdam, Holland, 42
Anderle, Dave, 83
Anka, Paul, 16
Any Old Way You Choose It: Rock and Other Pop Music, 1966-73 [book], 80
Asher, Tony, 33, 62-63
Bachman, R., 73
Barnes, Ken, 80
Barry, Jeff, 27, 61, 67, 71
Bates, L., 62
"The Beach Boys" [article], 81
The Beach Boys [book], 80, 82, 83,
Beach Boys 15th Anniversary Special [TV program], 9
"The Beach Boys: A California Saga" [article], 82, 84
The Beach Boys and the California Myth, [book], 82
Beach Boys...Twenty-Five Years Together [TV program], 8, 9
The Beach Boys: It's O.K. [TV program], 8
The Beatles, 13-14, 16-17, 22, 27, 29, 31-33, 36-37, 41, 51
Becher, C., 73
Belz, Carl, 80
Berlin, Irving, 60
Berry, Chuck, 15-16, 18, 21, 23-25, 29, 43, 56, 60, 71, 73
Berry, R., 59
Billboard [magazine], 6, 51, 53
Black musicians, 13, 15, 46
The Blackboard Jungle [film], 13
Blues shouter, 13
Brother Records, 6, 39, 64, 68, 69, 70
Brother/Reprise, 43, 68-69, 71-72
Bryant, B., 62
Buffalo Springfield, 31
Bugliosi, Vincent, 85
Burchman, B., 68
Burnett, Chester, 18
The Byrds, 31
California, 9, 10, 16-17, 19, 21, 35-36, 40, 42

California girl, 24
"California saga," 12
Campbell, Glenn, 6
Candix and X Records, 5, 20
Capehart, J., 55
Capitol Records, 5-7, 20, 39, 53, 55-67 74-78, 82
Capizzi, L., 60
Car songs, 22-24, 45, 80
Caribou Records, 53, 73, 75
Carnegie Hall, 7
Catalano, V., 55
CBS Records, 8, 53
Cervantes, 19
Chapin, B., 69-70
Charles, Ray, 18, 74
Chevy, 22
Christgau, Robert, 80
Christian, R., 56-58, 60, 62
Cleveland, Ohio, 8
The Coasters, 15
Cobb, E., 56
Cochran, E., 55
Cocktail [film], 8-9, 44
Cohn, Nik, 80
The Comets, 13
Concept album, 32, 41
Coots, J. F., 60
Cosby, H., 65
Couch, O., 57
Country-rock, 31
Country-Western, 13, 16
Crawdaddy [magazine], 7
Cream, 31
Crosby, Bing, 15
Crosby, Stills, Nash & Young, 31
Cruise, Tom, 44
Cushing-Murray, G., 73
Dale, D., 56, 60
Dante, 19
Del Mar, California, 21

Deuce Coupe [ballet], 7
Deuce Coupe II [ballet], 7
Doggett, B., 56
Doheny, California, 20, 21
The Doors, 31
Dorman, H., 62
Dragon, D., 69
Dylan, Bob, 18, 27, 29, 31, 37, 62
Eastern philosophy, 36
Edmonds, Ben, 81
Elliot, Brad, 55, 71, 81
Elvis: A Biography [book], 84
England, 6, 16, 31, 36, 52, 83
Faith, Percy, 28
Fassert, F., 62
The Fat Boys, 45-46, 77
Fataar, R., 69-70
Felton, David, 82
Fillmore Theater, 7
Fitzgerald, F. Scott, 85
The Flying Burrito Brothers, 31
Foster, S., 57, 74
The Four Freshmen, 21, 25
The Four Seasons, 28
Frazier, A., 60, 62
Freeman, B., 61
Gabree, John, 81
Gaines, Steven, 81
Gannon, K., 60
Gentry, Curt, 85
Gillespie, H., 60
Gillett, Charlie, 81
Girl singers, 15
Golden, Bruce, 9, 50, 104
Goldner, G., 58
Goldsmith, C., 62
The Grateful Dead, 7, 36
The Great Gatsby [book], 85
Greek poets, 18-19
Greenwich, Ellie, 27, 61, 67, 71

Haley, Bill, 13-14, 84
A Hard Day's Night [film], 27
Hardaway, 65
Harris, S., 60, 62
Harris' Department Store, 5
Hawthorne, California, 5, 83
Hay, R., 75
Hayes, B., 60
Help! [film], 27
Helter Skelter: The True Story of the Manson Murders [book], 85
Heroes and Villains: The True Story of the Beach Boys [book], 81
Hickey, E., 67, 74
Holland, 85
Holly, Buddy, 15, 72
Hopkins, Jerry, 84
Hopkins, John Henry, 60
House, Bill, 46, 77
Howling Wolf—see: Burnett, Chester
Instrumentals, 37
Instrumentation, 29, 34
It's Too Late To Stop Now: A Rock and Roll Journal [book], 81
Jacobson, G., 68, 73
Jahn, Mike, 81
Jan and Dean, 20
Jardine, Al, 5, 6, 9, 12, 38, 45, 57, 59, 61, 65-66, 68, 71-75 , 77
Jardine, L., 69
Jazz Dance: The Story of American Vernacular Dance [book], 84
"Jeffers County" [poem], 69
Jeffers, Robinson, 12, 69
Jefferson Airplane, 31, 36
Joffrey Ballet Company, 7
Johnson, J. W., 60
Johnson, Robert, 75, 84
Johnston, Bruce, 6, 9, 27, 38-40, 65, 67-68, 73-75, 77
Kalinich, S., 66
Kennedy, R., 69
Kent, W., 60
KFWB-Radio, 5
King, C., 71
King, Carol, 16

King, Martin Luther, 6
KMEN-Radio, 5
Knott, J., 68
Korthof, S., 66
Landau, Jon, 81
Landy, Eugene, 45, 49, 75, 77
Leaf, David, 82
Ledbetter, H., 67, 74
Leeds, M., 56
Leiber, J., 56, 68
Lennon, John, 27, 29, 62
Lewis, A., 71
Lewis, Jerry Lee, 14, 16
Lindsay, J., 75
Little Richard, 15-16, 25
Liverpool, England, 18
London Palladium, 78
Los Angeles, California, 21
Love, Mike, 5, 9, 12, 20, 27-28, 37, 40, 46, 55, 57-75, 77
Lymon, F., 58
The Machine in the Garden: Technology and the Pastoral Ideal in America, [book], 84
Malibu, California, 20
Malotte, A., 74
The Mamas and the Papas, 31, 49
Manson, Charles, 7, 39, 85
Marcus, Greil, 80, 84-85
Maresca, E., 60
Mareskola, 74
Marks, David, 5, 6
Marx, Leo, 84
May Day Antiwar Demonstration, 7
Mayorga, L., 56
McCartney, Paul, 27, 62
McDuff, E., 57
McKenzie, S., 77
Melcher, Terry, 46, 75, 77, 84
Milton, 19
Milward, John, 82
Mitchum, R., 57

Morgan, 78
Morgan, Alexandra, 45, 77
Morganfield, McKinley, 18
Motola, 74
Motown, 16, 37
Moy, S., 65
Muddy Waters—see: Morganfield, McKinley
Mystery Train: Images of America in Rock 'n' Roll Music [book], 80, 84
NBC-TV, 8
Nelson, S., 60
New Times [magazine], 7
New West [magazine], 8
Newsweek [magazine], 8
Nilsson, Harry, 31
Nolan, Tom, 82, 84
Norberg, B., 57, 59
Norman, 59
The Oaten Flute: Essays on Pastoral Poetry and the Pastoral Ideal [book], 84
O'Dowd, G. 75
Orbit Records, 78
Outlaw Blues: A Book of Rock Music [book], 83
Parks, J., 66
Parks, Van Dyke, 6, 37, 39, 41, 64, 67, 69
Parsons, Gram, 31
Pastoral theme, 18-19, 21-25, 28, 30, 32-33, 35-36, 40, 44-47, 50, 84-85
People [magazine], 7
Phillips, Cynna, 49
Phillips, John, 49, 77
Phillips, Michelle, 49
Pickett, B., 60
Poggioli, Renato, 84-85
Police Academy IV [film], 9
Pomus, D., 59
Preiss, Byron, 82
Presley, Elvis, 14-16, 25
Psychedelic movement, 36
Ram, B., 60

Rap music, 45, 46, 77
Raye, D., 57
Reagan, Ronald, 8, 10
Redondo Beach, California, 21
Rhythm-and-blues, 13, 37
Richie Valens Memorial Dance, 5
Rieley, Jack, 41, 68-70
Rimsky-Korsakov, 57
Ritz, L., 66
Robinson, Richard, 81
Rock Encyclopedia [book], 82
Rock: From Elvis Presley to the Rolling Stones [book], 81
Rock: From the Beginning [book], 80
Rock groups, 31
Rock 'n' Roll, 13-18, 22-23, 37-38, 43-46, 80, 84-85
Rock 'n' Roll Hall of Fame, 9
Rock Revolution [book], 81, 82
The Rockin' 50's [book], 84
Rolling Stone [magazine], 7, 8, 82, 84
The Rolling Stones, 16, 31, 81
Rollins, J., 56, 60
Roubanis, N., 56
Roxon, Lillian, 82
Russel, S.K., 56
Sachen, T., 63
San Bernardino, California, 5
San Bernardino Sun [newspaper], 85
San Francisco, California, 36, 83
San Onofre, California, 21
Scepter Records, 78
Schilling, M., 75
Schuman, M., 59
Sedaka, Neil, 16
Seldis, Paul David, 11, 104
Shakespeare, William, 19
Shaw, Arnold, 81-82, 84
Shaw, Greg, 80
Sherman, J., 60
Sherman, N., 60
The Silhouettes, 15

101

Simon and Garfunkel, 31
Smith, F., 62
The Sound of the City: The Rise of Rock and Roll [book], 81
Southern California, 12, 16-20, 23, 40, 47
Spector, Phil, 15-16, 27, 43, 61-62, 67, 71
Springboard Records, 78
Stars and Superstars of Rock [book], 83
Stearns, Marshall and Jean, 84
The Steve Allen Show [TV program], 14
Stoller, M., 56, 68
The Story of Rock [book], 80
Strezlecki, H., 60
The Surfaris, 77
Surf's Up: The Beach Boys on Record, 1961-1981 [book], 55, 81
Tate-LaBianca murders, 39
Tharp, Twyla, 7
Tin Pan Alley, 15-16
Titelman, T., 74
Tobler, John, 83
Troop Beverly Hills [film], 46
Troup, B., 58
Turner, Joe, 13
TV Guide [magazine], 8
Twist, 16
Tyrus, W. H., Jr., 61
Usher, G., 55-57, 59-60, 74
Valli, Franki, 28
Venet, Nick, 82
Ventura County, California, 21
Vescozo, A., 66
Village Voice [magazine], 8
Warner Brothers, 7, 8, 39, 53
Watt, James, 8, 10
Weaver, D., 55
White, C., 60, 62
Williams, Paul, 83
Wilson, Audree, 5
Wilson, Brian, 5, 7, 9-10, 18, 20-22, 24, 27-29, 32-41, 45, 49, 55-75, 77-78, 82-84
Wilson, Carl, 5, 9, 14, 39-41, 56, 59, 61, 65-70, 73, 75

Wilson, Carnie, 49
Wilson, Dennis, 5, 8-9, 38-39, 49, 57, 59, 61, 65-70, 73-74
Wilson, G., 57
Wilson, Murray, 5, 7, 82,
Wilson Phillips, 49
Wilson, R., Jr., 60, 62
Wilson, Wendy, 49
Winfrey, G., 68
Wise, F., 56
Wonder, S., 65, 75
Woody Woodpecker Symphony, 64
The World of Rock [book], 81
Yogi, Maharishi Mahesh, 6, 38,
Youth culture, 13

ABOUT THE AUTHORS

Bruce Golden is a Professor of English at California State University, San Bernardino. He has taught classes in rock music since 1970 and has been the recipient of National Endowment for the Humanities Awards for research in Renaissance Drama, and for Summer Fellowships for College Teachers. He has been coordinator for the English M.A. in Composition program, and he is the founder and director of the Center for Prose Studies at CSUSB. He has also published articles on Shakespeare, Lope de Vega, and Calderón.

Paul David Seldis is an editor at The Borgo Press as well as a freelance writer and journalist. While earning a B.A. in Creative Writing at the University of Arizona, he worked as an editorial and production assistant at the University of Arizona Press. He has written reviews on theater, film and photography exhibits, and on sports such as soccer and figure skating. His work has appeared in *The Tucson Weekly, Élan Magazine, Soccer America*, and in various newspapers in the Southwest. This is his first published book.

www.ingramcontent.com/pod-product-compliance
Lightning Source LLC
LaVergne TN
LVHW041633070426
835507LV00008B/593